Imagining
God throughout
Your Lifetime

God of Me

Rabbi David Lyon

For People of All Faiths, All Backgrounds
JEWISH LIGHTS Publishing
Woodstock, Vermont

God of Me:
Imagining God throughout Your Lifetime

2011 Quality Paperback Edition, First Printing
© 2011 by David Lyon

Library of Congress Cataloging-in-Publication Data
Lyon, David, 1962–
God of me : imagining God throughout your lifetime / David Lyon. — Quality paperback ed.
p. cm.
Includes bibliographical references.
ISBN 978-1-58023-452-8 (quality pbk. original)   1. God (Judaism)   I. Title.
BM610.L96 2011
296.3'1172—dc22

2010046399

10 9 8 7 6 5 4 3 2 1
Manufactured in the United States of America
Cover Design: Jenny Buono
Cover Art: © Phillip Jones / istockphoto.com
For People of All Faiths, All Backgrounds
Published by Jewish Lights Publishing
A Division of LongHill Partners, Inc.
Sunset Farm Offices, Route 4, P.O. Box 237
Woodstock, VT 05091
Tel: (802) 457-4000   Fax: (802) 457-4004
www.jewishlights.com

For Lisa,
Jeremy, Adam, Abby, and Emma.
They are reflections of my life's joy.

עָזִּי וְזִמְרָת יָהּ

The Eternal is my strength and might.
                    —Exodus 15:2

Contents

Acknowledgments

Since the time I was a young Jewish boy and I wrestled with God, I never fell out of faith with God. Over the years and into my rabbinate, I've discovered similar individuals who have wrestled with God and remained faithful, too. But I've also met individuals who have wrestled with God without much success at all. It is especially for them that this book has been written.

I am deeply indebted to the men and women who have served as my teachers, rabbis, and mentors. Rabbi Hillel Gamoran's gentle but confident presence served as a model for me when I was a young adult. He granted me my first students to tutor in Hebrew and my first classroom of Hebrew students. It would be the taste of teaching Judaism that would nourish my interests for a lifetime. I'm deeply grateful to my parents, Bob and Joyce Lyon, whose leadership in the synagogue and at home provided me a path into Jewish participation and identification.

The congregations I have served as rabbi provided me ample opportunities to meet Jewish children and adults on their Jewish journeys. Young and old, Reform and Conservative, they challenged me with their questions and needs. Over twenty years, the process helped me hone my own opinions and understanding, though they are always in formation.

At home in Houston and Congregation Beth Israel, I found my mentor, Rabbi Samuel E. Karff, who demanded of me no less than he demanded of himself. He has been a great role model who has confirmed for me that my role in the rabbinate has a special purpose and that the meaning of our work is truly sacred. Thankfully, the congregation he and I have served as senior rabbis cherishes that commitment.

In my personal home, there is no one who has supported me more than my dear wife, Lisa. Her patience, grace, and affection have sustained me through doubt and long hours, and in turn, we have sustained each other through shared joy and love. My children, Jeremy, Adam, Abby, and Emma are the dearest parts of my life. Their presence fills me up, and their dreams are part of the future I wish to share with them.

At the table where we study weekly, Rabbi Judith Abrams's encouragement compelled me to finish the book. I am very grateful. I thank my editor, Alys Yablon Wylen, whose skill helped me find my voice and write more deeply. I am also grateful to the team at Jewish Lights Publishing and its publisher, Stuart M. Matlins, with whom I shared many conversations during the process that ultimately brought this project to fruition.

Above all, I thank God for endowing me with a passion to search for truth, to seek justice, and to study Torah. My hope is that just as others have taught me, I may now teach you. To begin, we might say:

Baruch Atah, Adonai, Eloheinu Melech haolam, asher kideshanu bemitzvotav vetzivanu la'asok bedivrei Torah.

Blessed are You, Adonai, Sovereign of the universe, who sanctifies us with *mitzvot* and commands us to engage in Torah study.

יְיָ לִי וְלֹא אִירָא

God is with me;
I will not fear.
—Psalm 118:6

Introduction

There is no easy prescription for "how to know God." This book is founded on the principle that everyone can pursue a personal relationship with God, just as our patriarchs and matriarchs did in their lives. The central prayer in Jewish worship that highlights these relationships is called the *Amidah*, or *HaTefilah*, "The Prayer." The first part of *HaTefilah* is called *Avot v'Imahot* (Forefathers and Foremothers). It recognizes the personal relationship each of our ancestors had with God. It also recognizes the principle of *zechut avot v'imahot*, or the merit of our ancestors. The merit of our ancestors devolves upon us. As such, it also invites us to enjoy similar expectations for our own relationship with God. As God guided them, so God may guide us. As God loved them, so God may love us.

Thus, *Avot v'Imahot* is a carefully constructed formula that individualizes the relationship each of our patriarchs and matriarchs had with God, and which flows down to us:

> Praised are You, God, God of our fathers and mothers, God of Abraham, God of Isaac, God of Jacob, God of Sarah, God of Rebecca, God of Rachel, and God of Leah, great, mighty, and awesome God, God supreme. Master of all the living, Your ways are ways of love. You remember the faithfulness of our ancestors, and in love bring redemption to their children's children for the

sake of Your name. You are our Ruler and our Help, our Savior and our Shield. Blessed are You, God, the Shield of Abraham, the Helper of Sarah.

At first glance, it would be easy to reach the conclusion that the *Amidah* might actually be speaking of multiple gods. Each reference to God in relationship with a patriarch or matriarch could be describing separate ways in which they worshiped their own god. But, consistent with Jewish monotheism and Abraham's role as the first Jew, we just as easily reject the suggestion that the *Amidah* is recording the relationship of our ancestors with multiple gods. Our ancestors forged unique bonds with the One God.

The prayer's other purpose comes to light when it tells us that God "remember[s] the faithfulness of our ancestors," that is, their merit, and "in love bring[s] redemption" to their descendants. As God was for them, so God is "our Ruler and our Help, our Savior and our Shield." This is only the beginning of the section of the worship service called *HaTefilah*, but it is also the starting point from which all of us, descendants of our ancestors, can begin to lay claim to our own unique relationship to the One God.

Imagining God throughout Our Lives

In Judaism, there is no dogma. The closest we come to "dogma" is the principle of One God. Beyond that, how we come to imagine God is an individual endeavor. This does not mean that we are left to our own devices. It means that we have to be careful readers of Torah for evidence of the relationship we can have with God. It also means that we have to be good students of our Rabbis-of-old, who went on a similar journey into Torah for similar reasons. It is their insights and interpretations of Torah texts, called midrash, upon which we will rely for evidence of the relationship we can have with God.

The Rabbis' midrash show us how they stretched the boundary of inquiry by paying close attention to familiar and remarkable Torah texts in their effort to test their own faith in the One God. They held fast to their faith in One God, and their belief in God's omnipresence (God is everywhere), omniscience (God is all-knowing), and omnipotence (God is all-powerful), and used evidence in Torah text to make their points. They defended their conclusions about the divinity and eternality of God, and the finitude and temporality of humanity. They demonstrated that individual ways to imagine the One God, as our ancestors did, are not only possible, but also welcome.

The purpose of midrash on Torah, and the goals of the Rabbis who wrote them for us, are twofold: (1) to preserve the Torah's integrity as a sacred text by raising questions about what is written there and answering them, and (2) to teach moral lessons in order to provide enduring images of God's relationship with Israel.

In the chapters that follow, familiar and classic Torah texts and related Rabbinic midrash will open the way for mature God seekers to find God's presence in their life. The search begins in whatever time of life you find yourself, today. But it cannot exclude the past nor preclude the future. Therefore, the arc of this book will follow the progression of our understanding of and relationship with God, from the earliest ideas of a bearded Deity on a heavenly throne, to the mature image of God as a spiritual companion and source of comfort. We begin with a Torah text and midrash to establish God's omnipresence. Each subsequent text and midrash will guide us from childhood to maturity, with many stops along the way. By doing so, we will recall the years that have passed with greater insight into who we were on our way to becoming individuals in a unique relationship with God. In midlife, with the privilege of looking backward and ahead, we will find perspective on who we have become and who we might still be on our way to becoming. Ultimately, we will identify the source of our strength and appreciate the unique relationship we can develop with God from childhood to maturity.

God of Me

By virtue of the merit of our ancestors before God, we can have merit, too. This is where we, who seek a personal relationship with God, find our place in line. Now we can read the opening of the *Avot v'Imahot* prayer in a new way. Now we can read ourselves into it:

> Praised are You, God, God of our fathers and mothers, God of Abraham, God of Isaac, God of Jacob, God of Sarah, God of Rebecca, God of Rachel, God of Leah, *God of me.*

Without presumption, we add ourselves to a long list of Jewish men and women who come to experience God in their own way. Through authentic examination of Torah text and related midrash, we will cut through the preconceived ideas of God that we imagined in our childhood. We will break free from dogmas that we thought were real and that prohibited individuality. Like our ancestors and everyone who came between them and us, we can freely imagine the One God in our own way without violating any dogma. After all, how can we violate a dogma if it doesn't exist in the first place? The only commitment we need to make is to God who is One, not two (dual) or three (trinity). In addition, we have to agree that God is not none; in other words, we have to believe in the possibility of God.

For me, our greatest and most profound teachings come from Jewish sources combined with insights and experiences from real life. The Torah and midrash sometimes idealize life, but only to inspire us to reach for more in real circumstances.

The chapters that follow provide consistent and clear use of Torah and midrash to demonstrate that we can enjoy a unique relationship with God. Perhaps we have never known this relationship in the past, but we should not deprive ourselves of knowing it now. It is my hope that the journey you take while reading this book will lead you to the God of you.

About the Translations

Throughout the book, biblical texts are drawn from *Tanakh* (Philadelphia: Jewish Publication Society, 1985). These citations use gender language in reference to God. Rabbinical citations were cited in English from standard translations of Hebrew midrash (*Midrash Rabbah, Pesikta d'Rav Kahana,* et. al.), which use gender language in reference to God. Beyond biblical and rabbinical citations, every effort was made to preserve the readers' privilege to engage in the book's purpose by using gender-neutral language.

1

God Is Everywhere

*An angel of the Lord appeared to [Moses]
in a blazing fire out of a bush.*
—EXODUS 3:2

*No place is devoid of God's presence, not
even a thorn bush.*
—EXODUS RABBAH 2:5

A s we begin our new search for a unique relationship with God, one of the first things we must do is replace previously formed images of God from our childhood. When we were children, our parents, religious school teachers, and even gender-based prayer books led us to certain basic conclusions about God. These images become so basic to our understanding of God that they take time to alter and eventually erase.

God Is a Bearded King

Religious school teachers meant well even if they didn't teach us effectively or authentically about God. In children's services in the synagogue and lessons in the classroom, we heard standard prayers that confirmed what we learned. For example, the English translation of the words from Numbers 15:41, which make up the conclusion to the *Shema* in the worship service, conclude, "I am the Lord your God, who led you out of Egypt to be your God; I am the Lord your God." Children, who hear and understand ideas on a literal level, may well believe that the *rabbi* is God. After all, it is the rabbi who recites, "I am the Lord your God." So begins the image of God as the old man with a beard (at least in the instances where the rabbi was a man and wore a beard).

Our parents are often unprepared to teach us about God. In many cases, they are unprepared to imagine God for themselves in meaningful and unique ways. In many Jewish homes, parents do not read Hebrew comfortably and so they recite prayers only by rote. Often, questions their children ask them about God are answered unsatisfactorily with lofty words like "heaven" and "thrones of justice and mercy." Is it any wonder that many children never bring up the subject again? After all, they have been taught that God is an old, bearded man and beyond anyone's comprehension.

If we grew up anytime before the mid-1970s, then our prayer book was replete with male-gender language. We could not escape the assumption that God was King, Lord, He, and His. Only in the mid-1970s were any inroads made to begin imagining that God was truly without male form and gender. But it was still two decades before new prayer books in Reform and Conservative Judaism replaced for good any language that bound us to male images of God. New prayer books engage us in ways to imagine God through authentically gender-neutral language.

Preoccupied with other childhood interests, we accepted our elders' lessons, flawed as they were, and concluded that God was a man or a king, God was old and fat, God sat on a throne, and God was only up in the sky or in heaven. And although other ideas and outlooks on life tend to mature with time, these staid images of God often remain stubbornly and unfortunately rooted in our minds. Such a flawed God image impairs any hope that God's presence in our life could inspire us, guide us, and strengthen us. In a new search for God, our goals should be to bring down to earth this corpulent, monarchical deity and to find that God can be personal and unique to each of us.

A New Beginning

Our new search begins in the book of Exodus. In the story of Moses and the burning bush, we find the decisive moment when Moses found God in a most unremarkable place. The moment was prompted by critical circumstances. The Israelites were slaves in Egypt. Their spirits were crushed by cruel bondage. They had no hope for the future, and they began to believe that life without God would be their fate. Before Moses happened upon the burning bush, we read:

> The Israelites were groaning under the bondage [in Egypt] and cried out; and their cry for help from the bondage rose up to God. God heard their moaning, and God remembered [God's] covenant with Abraham, Isaac, and Jacob. God looked upon the Israelites, and God took notice of them.
>
> (Exodus 2:23–25)

God "took notice of them" because God remembered their ancestors, "Abraham, Isaac, and Jacob." *Zechut avot*, the merit of our ancestors, was an active principle at work even then, and it afforded Moses and the Israelites a place in God's covenant. What follows immediately in Torah is the moment God called Moses into service and Moses responded:

Now Moses, tending the flock of his father-in-law Jethro, the priest of Midian, drove the flock into the wilderness, and came to Horeb, the mountain of God. An angel of the Lord appeared to him in a blazing fire out of a bush. He gazed, and there was a bush all aflame, yet the bush was not consumed. Moses said, "I must turn aside to look at this marvelous sight; why doesn't the bush burn up?" When the Lord saw that he had turned aside to look, God called to him out of the bush: "Moses! Moses!" He answered, "Here I am." And [God] said, "Do not come closer. Remove your sandals from your feet, for the place on which you stand is holy ground. I am," [God] said, "the God of your father, the God of Abraham, the God of Isaac, and the God of Jacob." And Moses hid his face, for he was afraid to look at God.

(Exodus 3:1–6)

Moses had never known or experienced the God of Israel in this way. It was a new and sudden experience he had trouble comprehending. He said, "I must turn aside to look at this marvelous sight; why doesn't the bush burn up?" (Exodus 3:3). When God saw that Moses had turned aside, God called to him from out of the bush (or thorn bush, as described in midrash) by name, seeking him out. God chose Moses to lead the Israelites out of Egypt because of his cherished status as God's faithful servant. Only as free people could the Israelites enjoy for themselves "*zechut avot v'imahot*," the merit of their ancestors, and begin to build their own relationship with God. In response to God's call, Moses answered, *Hineini*, "Here I am" (Exodus 3:4).

This is the first time in the Torah that God's presence appears in an inanimate object. Abraham, Isaac, and Jacob were all called by God and visited by God's angels or messengers, but only Moses came upon a manifestation of God, and it was in a place no one would have expected. After all, God showed up in a scrappy bush, not a beautiful thing in nature. In childhood, we were taught to use positive images and grand expectations when we thought of God. Whether we worshiped in religious school or on Shabbat, the prayers we recited to God were filled with praise and thanksgiving. Only if we prayed during the week would we have included petitionary and intercessory prayers. Is the Torah flawed? Is this the God to whom the Israelites directed their pleas and the God we are searching for today? That's precisely the question raised by the Rabbis in their midrash on this Torah text. Their interpretation could be our first reliable answer since childhood on the subject of God's presence and our first step toward a new image of God's presence in our life.

Understanding the Burning Bush

Focusing on the verse that includes the words "out of the bush" (Exodus 3:4), the Rabbis asked the obvious question, "Why did God choose a thorn bush from which to appear before Moses?" Their midrash provided the answer:

> A heathen once asked Rabbi Joshua ben Korchah, "Why did God choose a thorn bush from which to speak to Moses?" He replied, "Were it a carob tree or a sycamore tree, you would have asked the same question; but to dismiss you without any reply is not right, so I will tell you why. To teach you that no place is devoid of God's presence, not even a thorn bush."
>
> (Exodus Rabbah 11:5)

The purpose of the midrash was to reveal important insights into God's presence in this familiar Torah text. The lesson in the midrash and the conclusion the Rabbis reached provide textual proof that God is not only up in heaven. God is everywhere.

The midrash begins with a heathen (nonbeliever) who is pitted against a knowledgeable and wise rabbi. The Rabbis assumed that a nonbeliever would have doubted God's presence under any circumstances. The nonbeliever would have doubted the veracity of the Torah story whether God appeared in something beautiful, like a sycamore tree, or something simple, like a thorn bush. In fact, the midrash assumes that no one is without some religious doubt, including the Rabbis themselves, who perfected their own faith only after they challenged it, too. Presumably, they challenged their own faith while remaining confident that the conclusion would, indeed, perfect their faith and not diminish it. By extending their reach to any and all nonbelievers, no matter their issue, they reached a boundary wherein they taught that God was unfailingly omnipresent.

To make their point, the Rabbis used contrasting symbols. Unlike carob trees and sycamore trees, which are beautiful, the thorn bush is scrappy. Carob is a substitute for chocolate, and it grows well in the Middle East. A sycamore tree has large branches and offers welcome shade. These trees are so beautiful that some people landscape their yards with them. But nobody landscapes their yards with thorn bushes, even if they claim to be firm believers in biblical stories.

Our own contemporary impulse would be at least the same as the nonbeliever's, who demanded to know, "Why does God choose to appear in something lowly instead of something desirable?" The Rabbis' conclusion about God's omnipresence was a reasonable and reasoned one: "If God could appear in a lowly thing, then God could surely appear anywhere, including something spectacular."

Now, let's test their conclusion by reimagining the God of our childhood. In that simple and basic time of our life, we could only see the world as children see it: for what it was and for what it was not. It was good and evil. It was kind and mean. It was right and wrong. It was beautiful and ugly. Thus, the challenge for us as children was finding God in both good and evil, in beauty and ugliness, all at the same time. It was nearly impossible for us to imagine on our own.

Drawing on the Rabbis' midrash, we can look back into our childhood and see that God's presence really was everywhere. It was in good and evil, and it was in beauty and ugliness. Let's start with good and beauty.

A simple childhood experience is a family vacation, a time of recreation with parents and siblings, in a setting usually far from home and familiar surroundings. The expectation of parents was to expose their children to new and different sights and experiences. The effect was almost always achieved.

When we stood on that mountainside or on that seashore for the first time, we thought to ourselves or shouted aloud freely, "Oh my God, this is so beautiful!" When we returned home and viewed the grand pictures of those tremendous mountains or seashores, they evoked similar responses.

When we remarked, "Oh my God!" we probably thought that we were just making a large statement about what we saw or experienced. Without the capacity to label it a theological comment, we were merely reaching as far as we could with the words we had come to know. But, in reality, the remark "Oh my God!" even when we said it in childhood, was the beginning of a profound statement about our relationship to nature and its Creator. Everything about the words "Oh my God!" reflected our recognition that *we* alone did not create this remarkable sight. Something larger than us, God, was responsible for what we observed.

Experiences on the mountain or at the seashore awakened us to our surroundings as children and our place in them. Just as God created us, so God created the natural world we came on vacation to enjoy. Or, put conversely, just as God created the natural world we came to enjoy on vacation, so God created something equally "awesome" in us.

Our parents modeled what they could for us about God. But their limited experience and their inability to convey authentic lessons to us confounded our development. On that mountaintop or seashore, it was the rare parent who recited *Shehecheyanu*, a prayer of gratitude, or took time to attach their children's awesome experience to the role that God played in creating that place or that experience. They didn't destroy their children's chance at attaching their own awareness of God's place there, but they didn't advance it either by demonstrating their own adult image of God's presence there.

The risk of relying on mountains and seashores to observe God's presence is that we might conclude God is only present in beautiful places. To attach our understanding of God's presence to those beautiful places, alone, deepens our misunderstanding of God's presence, which belongs to all places.

Surely, God is also present in the soup kitchen or the depressed urban area we visited or passed through with our parents. The challenge is that as children we often failed to make the same connection between God and impoverished settings as we did on the top of the mountain. God wasn't absent in those places, but parents who protected their children or sheltered them from broader life experiences also prevented them from making their own connections between God's presence and places where real suffering and hardship exist.

Finding God in the Rubble

There are times when long-held childhood images of God are shaken. They force us to see God where we need God to be. In April 2006, just seven months after Hurricane Katrina wreaked havoc on New Orleans, a group of Jewish professional and lay leaders organized by the Union for Reform Judaism went on a fact-finding trip to New Orleans and surrounding areas. At the time, there was no place like it on earth. It was a place where a natural disaster created a real boundary between good and evil, beauty and ugliness, prosperity and adversity. The purpose of the trip was to assess the damage and bring home data that would direct resources to the people and institutions that needed them most. To any observer, the damage was catastrophic. Seven months after the hurricane there was still more evidence of disaster than relief, and the question of where to begin was just coming into focus.

The visiting group recalled the biblical story of the spies, Joshua and Caleb, who scouted out the new land before the Israelites entered it:

> When Moses sent them to scout the land of Canaan, he said to them, "Go up there into the Negev and on into the hill country, and see what kind of country it is. Are the people who dwell in it strong or weak, few or many? Is the country in which they dwell good or bad? Are the towns they live in open or fortified? Is the soil rich

or poor? Is it wooded or not? And take pains to bring
back some of the fruit of the land."

(Numbers 13:17–20)

Despite the challenges they knew were present in the land, Joshua
and Caleb brought back an inspiring report that encouraged the
people that God's presence was among them, even there:

> At the end of forty days they returned from scouting the
> land. They went straight to Moses and Aaron and the
> whole Israelite community … and made their report.…
> This is what they told him: "We came to the land you
> sent us to; it does indeed flow with milk and honey, and
> this is its fruit. However, the people who inhabit the
> country are powerful, and the cities are fortified and
> very large.…" Caleb hushed the people before Moses
> and said, "Let us by all means go up, and we shall gain
> possession of it, for we shall surely overcome it."
>
> (Numbers 13:25–30)

The report inspired the Israelites to believe that a better life was
waiting for them in the Promised Land. This was the message that
the "scouts" in New Orleans brought home with them.

God's presence was with the people of New Orleans, in precisely the places they found hope. Now, the words "Oh my God!"
evoked deep feelings by those who saw the city at its best and its
worst. There was no mistaking the fact that God's presence could
be found at once in both the spared parts of the city and the most
devastated sections.

God's presence was found in the hope people discovered in
community centers. Their lives as they knew them were washed
away with the floodwaters. Literally, their homes and businesses

were washed away like nothing more than the sticks and boards that held them loosely together for so many years. With them went their families and friends who were displaced and struggling to return. But, in conversations about their plight, they spoke words of faith. Despite massive losses, they believed that God's presence inspired them to find within themselves the vast resources that would enable them to rebuild their communities and remake their lives. Precisely in the crisis and the devastation that would take years to overcome in New Orleans, God's presence was found.

Hineini: Here I Am

The mountaintop and the seashore, the soup kitchen and the devastation in New Orleans, are all physical places where God's presence can be found. Moving beyond physical places, there is still another, more personal place where we would hope to find God, in both good and bad times. It's in each of us. Children experience many emotions but tend to need help expressing them. Eventually, children learn how to calm themselves, which puts them in control of how they choose to feel about events and experiences. Children learn that happiness is something they can attain no matter how parents or others treat them. Likewise, sadness is something they may choose to feel even in the middle of a birthday party. Quicker than parents know it, children learn to choose their own feelings, which leads them, as they grow up, to choose their own worldview.

The Rabbis' midrash is perfectly suited to help us take ownership of our feelings and our increasingly adult image of God. There were times in our lives—peak moments or joyful experiences—when we felt beautiful like a sycamore tree. It was then that we felt popular. We felt lucky. Maybe we even felt blessed.

Like the midrash, in those moments we didn't deny God's presence. They were times when we likely said, "Thank God!" or "I feel special." Even if we didn't pause to give thanks to God, either because we didn't know how or because our parents didn't lead us in prayer at home, it's possible that we still didn't take complete credit for our special feelings, either. We probably thanked our parents or our teachers because they represented the most authoritative figures we knew in our lives at the time. If we did thank God, even in a childlike way, we did it because we had good role models in our life and they showed us how and why to give thanks. We felt blessed because we felt lucky. Even if we knew little about God, we attached ourselves to the part we could understand or were willing to acknowledge.

Unfortunately, life isn't always like the sycamore or carob trees that represent only joy. Soon enough, children know that there are many days filled with some tears. When we hurt, we are like a thorn bush. Eventually, we also come to know that we resemble a thorn bush more often than we do a sycamore or carob tree. When we feel ugly, unwanted, disappointed, or frustrated, we wonder where God is. Our emotional low points stand in the way of our faith and hope that God is still with us. Indeed, God is present in these low times, but not for the same reasons God was with us when we felt as beautiful as a sycamore or carob tree.

In the midst of sadness, we don't feel inclined to give thanks to God, no matter how faithful we might be. Some say that we suffer for a reason. Perhaps, but suffering is not a virtue in Judaism, even if it teaches us something about life and living. Remember the motto "No pain, no gain"? Now, consider the motto "No pain, no pain." When we suffer, we would prefer to know that God, like an unconditionally loving parent, is present as a source of courage, comfort, and hope. When we suffer, the last thing we need is the one who caused our suffering to stand over us and say, "There, you needed that!" No, we didn't. Children need to know that even though life can be hard, God can also be like a loving parent who eases their pain.

Most children heal from their hurts. Their skinned knees mend on their own with a good bandage. A parent's kiss still speeds healing. But there are broken times in children's lives that cannot be easily mended or covered up. A parent's kiss can only do so much to reassure a sad or frightened child.

One of the strangest and saddest experiences for children is a funeral. When children attend their first funeral, they are struck by the strange events and difficult emotions of the adults around them. Parents who, themselves, never experienced the death of a close family member are unprepared to comfort their children appropriately. Parents whose own God images are stuck in their childhood have nothing to draw on when their children ask why everyone is sad and who's in the box. Once, a young parent holding his daughter by the casket explained to her that grandpa was in the "box" and that he would travel to heaven in it. Imagine the child's horror when the box was placed in the ground and covered over with dirt. Even a child knows that a box can't get to heaven if it's covered with all that dirt.

Children are literal. This child would have been comforted had she been told that while her grandfather's body went into the earth, the way she remembered him lives on. She would also have been comforted if she was told that her grandpa's soul returns to God, who gave it to him when he was born. She would have learned from her own father's sadness how to mourn without losing control. She would have been comforted knowing that even though she couldn't see her grandpa again, she could still think of him anytime she wanted to or look at pictures at home when she missed him. The father would have provided a lifelong lesson to his daughter had he said that God mourned with her, too.

Like Moses who happened upon a bush that burned unconsumed and for whom God remembered the covenant God made with Abraham, Isaac, and Jacob, God's presence is found in all the times of our life, whether they are happy or sad and whether they are beautiful or simple places. Our hope that we can find God in all the times of our life cannot be pinned to mountains and seashores. The nonbeliever in the midrash was not just a visitor to a wise rabbi. He was the perennial doubter within us who returns, even in times of joy, to raise questions about God's presence.

In our Torah text, Moses stumbled upon the burning bush. He approached it cautiously. He stood in awe of it because it burned without being consumed. He didn't throw sand on it to extinguish it. He beheld the extraordinary sight. But let's not forget that God, manifested in that burning bush, also beheld a marvelous sight. God saw Moses and called out to him, "Moses, Moses!" and Moses replied to him, "Here I am!" It was a spectacular beginning to an enduring relationship. As it was for Moses, finding God in all the times of our life also depends on our ability to hear the still small voice within us and the wisdom to reply, *Hineini*, "Here I am!"

2

God Loves Me

"Hurry down, for your people, whom you brought out of the land of Egypt, have acted basely."

—Exodus 32:7

"Be they sinful or virtuous, they are Yours."

—Pesikta d'Rav Kahana 128b

We were created in God's image. Torah tells us, "And God created man in [God's] image, in the image of God, [God] created him; male and female [God] created them" (Genesis 1:27). As God's own creation, God's love for us is unconditional and enduring. Therefore, we anticipate that God's love will be demonstrated in acts of merciful compassion and remarkable patience, even under trying circumstances. In fact, God's love for us does grow deeper as it develops through experience.

Just as we begin to assert our independence in adolescence and to rebel against our parents, our image of God can be blurred by confusion. If God is only a parentlike figure who rewards and punishes, then our relationship with God will need time and clarification, too. Adolescents, preteens and teenagers, test their parents. They want to individuate from their parents, but they also count on their parents to provide safe boundaries in which they can learn about themselves as they grow up. This transition requires extraordinary patience and unconditional love from parents. Similarly, at precisely this time when we need a confidant in our life with whom to share our fears and our hopes, God can show us extraordinary patience and unconditional love. God is a source of everything we need while we're growing up and discovering more about our unique personality, our awkwardness, and our dreams.

The Golden Calf

In no other biblical story are the struggles of adolescence better exemplified than in the transformative journey the Israelites took out of Egypt. At this time, the Israelites were like rebellious children who desperately wanted to be loved, to be free, and to feel secure. Exodus 32 relates one of the most memorable events in Israelite history and one of the most moving examples of God's unconditional love deepening through experience. We begin with Exodus 31:18, where we read, "When God finished speaking with him [Moses] on Mount Sinai, [God] gave Moses the two tablets of the Pact, stone tablets inscribed with the finger of God." Then Moses turned to head down the mountain to deliver God's words to the Israelite people:

> When the people saw that Moses was so long in coming down from the mountain, the people gathered against Aaron and said to him, "Come, make us a god who shall go before us, for that man Moses, who brought us from the land of Egypt, we do not know what has happened to him." Aaron said to them, "Take off the gold rings that are on the ears of your wives, your sons, and your

daughters, and bring them to me." And all the people took off the gold rings that were in their ears and brought them to Aaron. This he took from them and cast in a mold, and made it into a molten calf. And they exclaimed, "This is your god, O Israel, who brought you out of the land of Egypt!" When Aaron saw this, he built an altar before it; and Aaron announced: "Tomorrow shall be a festival of the Lord!" Early next day, the people offered up burnt offerings and brought sacrifices of well-being; they sat down to eat and drink, and then rose to dance.

The Lord spoke to Moses, "Hurry down, for your people, whom you brought out of the land of Egypt, have acted basely. They have been quick to turn aside from the way that I enjoined upon them. They have made themselves a molten calf and bowed low to it and sacrificed to it, saying: 'This is your god, O Israel, who brought you out of the land of Egypt!'"

(Exodus 32:1–8)

Upon seeing the Israelites' sin forged in the Golden Calf, God further said to Moses:

"Now, let Me be, that My anger may blaze forth against them and that I may destroy them, and make of you a great nation."

(Exodus 32:10)

But Moses implored God:

"Let not Your anger, O Lord, blaze forth against Your people, whom You delivered from the land of Egypt with great power and with a mighty hand. Let not the

Egyptians say, 'It was with evil intent that [God] delivered them, only to kill them off in the mountains and annihilate them from the face of the earth.' Turn from Your blazing anger, and renounce the plan to punish Your people. Remember Your servants, Abraham, Isaac, and Israel [Jacob], how You swore to them Your Self and said to them: I will make your offspring as numerous as the stars of heaven, and I will give to your offspring this whole land of which I spoke, to possess forever."

And the Lord renounced the punishment [God] had planned to bring upon [God's] people.

(Exodus 32:11–14)

It's critical to note that at the beginning of the book of Exodus, after God singled out Moses and his brother, Aaron, God sent them to Pharaoh with an order. They were commanded to tell Pharaoh, "Thus says the Lord, the God of the Hebrews: 'Let My people go, that they may celebrate a festival for Me in the wilderness'" (Exodus 5:1). Through signs and portents sent by God through Moses, the Egyptians suffered the Ten Plagues as Pharaoh's heart hardened against God. The familiar story of Israelite suffering ended when they were redeemed by God's awesome might. They made their way through the Sea of Reeds on dry land, while the Egyptian soldiers "sank like lead" (Exodus 15:10) into the waters. Then, still long before the Israelites came to the Promised Land, they arrived at Mount Sinai. There they waited for Moses to return from meeting God atop the mountain. Days went by and the people, now tired from their journey and losing faith, began to doubt whether Moses would ever return. They began to fall back on what they knew from Egypt. They abandoned any chance of faith in God, whom they couldn't see, in favor of pagan idols they could see. Eventually, they sought comfort in the construction of a Golden Calf, a pagan god and an affront to the God of Israel.

Now let's look closely at the Torah verses cited in this chapter to see what the Rabbis observed. When Moses went to Pharaoh, he said on God's behalf, "Let *My* people go!" Moses and Aaron were God's mouthpieces. They acted as prophets before Pharaoh. But later, when the Israelites were engaged in building the Golden Calf, God said to Moses, "Hurry down, for *your* people, whom you brought out of the land of Egypt, have acted basely" (Exodus 32:7). What happened? When the Israelites were good, they belonged to God? When the Israelites were evil, they belonged to Moses?

This is the same conversation that takes place between parents when their children have misbehaved or made an error in judgment. When they're good, they're "our children," and when they're bad, they're "your children." It's a terribly confusing exchange that pits parents and children against each other and leaves everyone insecure. The midrash removes the insecurity between God and the Israelites and restores their unconditional relationship. The Rabbis teach us how Moses helped preserve the relationship between God and the Israelite people. One midrash in particular uses an analogy to illustrate how the covenant was durable and God's love was unconditional:

> Rabbi Berechiah, in the name of Rabbi Levi, said: A king had a vineyard that he entrusted to a tenant. When the wine was good, he said, "How good is the wine of my vineyard." When it was bad, he said, "How bad is the tenant's wine." The tenant said, "Be the wine good or bad, it is yours." So, at first, God said to Moses, "I will

send you to Pharaoh that he may let My people go." But after the making of the Golden Calf, God said, "Go, get down, for your people have corrupted themselves." Moses said, "So, then, when they sin, they are mine; when they are virtuous, they are Yours. Not so; be they sinful or virtuous, they are Yours."

(*Pesikta d'Rav Kahana* 128b)

The analogy is perfect. The king is God. The tenant is Moses. The wine is the Israelite people. The midrash doesn't teach every detail of the analogy; that is left for students of midrash to consider. For example, the "stiffnecked people" (Exodus 32:9) are compared to the wine. Winemakers know that small details that are often out of their control can affect the quality of the grapes they use to make their wine every season. Climate, water, fertilizer, and care are all part of the challenge of making award-winning wine. The stiffnecked people to whom God referred in Exodus 32:9 shared all the characteristics of wine, which depends on many variables.

The Rabbis, therefore, distilled down the essence of the covenantal relationship between God and Israel. Just as the owner and not the tenant must take ultimate responsibility for the product of his fields, so God must take ultimate responsibility for the Israelite people. What's more, the Rabbis never doubted that it would be the outcome. Long after the incident of the Golden Calf, the covenant endured. So, the midrash teaches us not that the covenant was on the brink of destruction, but rather that it is remarkably durable. There is no other explanation for Moses's retort, "So, then, when they sin [and they will], they are mine; when they are virtuous, they are Yours. Not so; be they sinful or virtuous, they are Yours."

The relationship between God and Moses did more than endure. It provided the strength for the relationship between God and the Israelites to endure, too. The Rabbis understood that at this point, the relationship could stand up to formidable tests only if it were founded on the covenant God made with Abraham, Isaac, and Jacob. The relationship would grow through Moses, who would provide the means by which the Israelites would come to know God then and for all time. Indeed, God was a God of justice and mercy and One who loved them unconditionally under all circumstances.

God as Parent

To this day, Judaism recognizes that God's unconditional love enables us to strive for human improvement without fear of losing God's love in our attempt. We can stumble even as we seek life, make decisions, and improve our lot, and we can do it in a trusting and benevolent relationship with God.

To highlight God's unique and unconditional love for Israel, we can liken it to the love parents have for their teenage children. Think about the bond between parents and their teenagers when it is at its best. Parents adore their children and provide them with nourishment, both physically and emotionally. But even they cannot always save their children from harm or even from harming themselves. Though children might complain that their parents didn't love enough, it can still be said, more often than not, that even when parents didn't give love easily, they meant well anyway, and when they didn't give their children what they wanted, they gave them what they thought they needed instead.

The same can be said for God's love for us. God loves us dearly, as God's own creation. Even so, God cannot keep us from harm or even from harming ourselves. God can comfort and console us. God can rejoice with us and bless us. God's love is also deeper than we may be ready to acknowledge, and our lot in life may be more than we have discovered. A relationship with God, like one with our parents, evolves. It changes. It has to.

To every teenager, what's fair and true is still to be sorted out. For now, answers lie more with their peers than they do with their parents or with God. Adolescence exposes them to life through movies, world news, and conversations they will inevitably have with their peers and their parents. Tough questions follow tough issues. Their search for truth will bring them to sources of wisdom that have stood the test of time and faith. Now is the time for teenagers to avail themselves of Judaism's wisdom about a world they are just beginning to know.

Why versus How

Teenagers who are participating in the world increasingly on their own terms will hear confusing messages about the way God acts in our life. For example, some years ago at the winter holiday season, the television news reported that an accident claimed the life of a teenager. The clergyperson present at the scene asked despondently, "Why? Why now?" From a Jewish perspective, it was an odd question. The question "why" can never be answered satisfactorily, because no one knows with absolute certainty why such tragedies occur, ill-timed as they are. Some explain that the death of a young person means that God needed him or her more than he or she was needed in this world. Judaism rejects such an assumption and emphasizes that God's commandments, *mitzvot*, can only be fulfilled in life. God loves us. So, God mourns with us, too.

For teenagers, who are prone to believe in their own immortality, news of a peer's tragic death is alarming. That God "needed"

a young person more than did his parents or life itself is confusing at a time when their image of God is still in formation. At
best, they need God to confirm that their life is valued and valu-
able and that their purpose in living is still ahead of them in this
world.

The second question posed by the clergyperson, "Why now?"
might presume that if it happened in June and not December, it
would have been better. There is no time that is better for a
tragedy. Judaism holds that a tragedy is not the absence of God's
love, no less than a parent's love is absent when he or she closes a
door on a child's finger or stands helplessly as a child stumbles
into harm's way. The intersection of events is not without God's
love. God is like a loving parent. God cannot manipulate events
any more than parents can manipulate a perfect future for their
child. Tragedy happens. Life is hard and God's love endures. "Why
does tragedy happen?" is a stubborn question that cannot be easily answered.

However, Judaism doesn't deprive us of asking a meaningful
question. Instead of asking "why," Judaism teaches us to ask
"how." "How" is linked to the book of Lamentations, the Hebrew
word for which is *Eichah*, or "how." In tragedy, we ask how an event
happened, how we can prevent it from happening again, and how
we can begin again. Our ability to cope and participate in life as we
once did is a sign of personal strength. It's also a sign of increasing
awareness of God's love.

This is especially important for adolescents who are, by their
nature, struggling to order their world for themselves. When
tragedy happens, their ability to answer questions about it reason-
ably and rationally will not preclude them from responding to it
with increasing faith, too. God's unconditional love is not absent,
but it does serve a unique purpose during trying times. When

teenagers experience it appropriately, they will grow up and be transformed for a lifetime.

In Judaism, when death occurs we are taught to say, "Blessed are You, God, Judge of Truth." Truth is capitalized to reflect a truth that only God knows, but which serves us in the presence of a fully loving God. The blessing restores our trust that despite life's fragility we can affirm God's love for us. God's love in our life assures us that chaos will not prevail even when tragedy leads us to believe that all is lost or broken irreparably. The measure of our strength is how we overcome adversity. We begin with assurances of God's love for us.

Unconditional Love

Adolescents' lessons with unconditional love are often learned on their own terms. It is not uncommon for their first experiences to come from the relationships they have with pets and other animals. It's the first time they're in control of setting boundaries and giving or withholding praise or criticism. Parents are often moved by their teenagers' displays of adult behavior when caring for animals. They should be, because they're modeling what they have observed at home, and they're making it their own.

Teenagers often relate to stories about animals and especially puppies. Their vulnerability reminds them instinctively of their own, so they tend to them thoughtfully and lovingly. When my family acquired its first puppy, we named him Buddy. He was a new two-and-a-half-pound Cavalier King Charles spaniel. At night, the dog refused to sleep in his kennel downstairs and away from the rest of the family. He barked and he banged on the slim bars that held him captive. Eventually, I had no choice but to retrieve him from his veritable prison. When I opened the kennel door, he jumped into my arms and aimed for my face. He thanked me with a wet tongue that coated my ear, neck, and face. Lying back in a chair, it went on for what seemed forever, and then it suddenly stopped! I thought, what happened, did he run out of water? Exhausted, the puppy fell asleep on my neck. You can imagine the tender scene. About animals, the German-American scholar and twentieth-century Jewish theologian Martin Buber said, "An animal's eyes have the power to speak a great language." And, apparently, so does its tongue.

Of course, teenagers learn about love and boundaries not only from their parents and their pets. If nearly 50 percent of marriages end in divorce, then many adolescents' experience with love and boundaries are being shaped under trying circumstances. They know more than anyone what it means to find love and boundaries away from their parents. Sometimes, at best, they find it in the company of grandparents or foster parents.

As adopted children come to know, parents are not necessarily the ones who bore them. More often, the bonding relationship occurs between children and the adults who love and protect them. Together, they grow up to discover more about themselves and the world around them. The power of unconditional love for adolescents cannot be underestimated. It is related to the value they place on their own life. Love at an early and formative time in their life helps them feel loved and lovable by others and by God for the duration.

In Reform congregations, it is customary for sophomores in high school to study with their rabbis in confirmation class. Unlike their bar or bat mitzvah year, confirmation is a time when students are more likely to study thoughtfully and deeply on subjects that concern them. In my confirmation classes, students learn to understand their images of God. Every year, without fail, one student emerges with questions that go beyond the scope of the class and his or her peers. The student, more often a boy than a girl, makes time to visit with me and to ask specific questions. The student is intelligent. In school, he is typically interested in history and literature. Now, Judaism raises questions he's been thinking about recently.

In one meeting, such a student wanted to know how God could be proved. In his science classes at school, empirical data and the scientific method taught that only that which could be replicated in a laboratory setting could be true. God cannot be proved by the scientific method; therefore, what was he supposed to do with God in an empirical world? It was time to introduce him to modern theologians who could answer his question about God, without upsetting the laws of science he so respected.

Martin Buber, I briefly explained to him, taught that God could not be proved or defined. God could only be encountered through meetings where we and another are in a completely accepting relationship. Within that moment of fully accepting another person, we find God's presence as well as significant self-knowledge. In a fully accepting relationship, we learn how caring, thoughtful, and empathetic we can be. When we meet others and engage in a fully accepting relationship, even if it's momentary, we discover more about ourselves and the meaning of being created in God's image.

For adolescents, this is an important gateway to mature relationships. At some point, they grow dependent on but also weary of superficial friendships that focus only on clothing, sports, and gossip. Best friends and lasting memories will thrive on times and events where fully accepting oneself and another builds understanding, empathy, and real love.

Because Judaism is not dogmatic, in another meeting I offered the same student a lesson on Rabbi Milton Steinberg, a twentieth-century scholar. He was known as a limited theist. He believed that God was all-loving but not all-powerful. The student was interested in this theology. As a teenager, he felt strongly that God did not direct his life. He believed that he had much more to say about his own present and future. Nevertheless, he believed that God had something to do with his life and the way it might unfold. On subjects such as grades and success, he believed that he was fully in charge of his destiny. Even on subjects of love and marriage, he believed that he was fully in charge. It wasn't until we talked about world peace or hope that he began to relinquish some control to God. Not surprisingly, he enjoyed the power and authority he was learning how to use in his life, separate from his parents and other authority figures. To him, God was an authority figure, too; but, like his relationship with his parents, he didn't want to excuse God—he merely wanted to let God in when he was ready or needed God most. Fair enough. He was now armed with ideas about God that would enable him to grow his relationship with God as he traversed adolescence.

The hope he had in God's presence in his life was not about perfect faith. It was about God's unconditional love. He needed to know that while he found his way in the world on his own terms, despite inevitable pitfalls and mistakes, God would be there. He wanted to know that he could retrieve God when he needed, and he wanted me to know that he didn't take the relationship for granted. He just needed some time and some space.

From Theory to Practice

The law of the leper (found in Leviticus 14) says much about both the Rabbis of the midrash and us, who want to live with God's love at home and in the community:

The Lord spoke to Moses, saying: This shall be the ritual
for a leper [*metzora*] at the time that he is to be cleansed.

(Leviticus 14:1)

When the person's infirmity was reported to the priest, the priest
examined the flesh. If he was a *metzora*, he was moved outside the
camp. Later, if he was healed, he returned after making appropriate offerings to God. In such times, the whole community was
affected by the risk that this man's uncleanness would prevent
God's blessings from reaching them. But whose fault was it? What
exactly was the problem that biblical translations call "leprosy"?
This discoloration in the skin that made a person unclean and
infectious was not clearly understood. If it was a punishment
from God, as they would have imagined in their time, what was
the punishable deed that could lead to such hardship for the individual and such a threat to the community? The Rabbis performed their own examination—not on the skin this time, but
rather on the Torah text.

In Leviticus 14:1, they read the Hebrew word *metzora* and
taught the following in a midrash:

The law of the leper is alluded to in what is written,
"Who is the one who desires life?" (Psalm 34:13). This
may be compared to the case of the peddler who used to
go around the towns in the vicinity of Sepphoris, crying
out, "Who wishes to buy the elixir of life?" and drawing
great crowds around him. Rabbi Jannai was sitting and
expounding in his room and heard him calling out,
"Who desires the elixir of life?" He said to him, "Come
here, and sell me it." The peddler said, "Neither you nor
people like you require that which I have to sell." The
rabbi pressed him, and the peddler went up to him and

brought out the book of Psalms and showed him what is written immediately thereafter: "Keep your tongue from evil; depart from evil and do good" (Psalm 34:14–15). Rabbi Jannai said, "Solomon, too, proclaims, 'Whoever keeps his mouth and his tongue keeps his soul from troubles' (Proverbs 21:23)." Rabbi Jannai said, "All my life have I been reading this passage, but did not know how it was to be explained, until this peddler came and made it clear to me."

"Who is the one who desires life? Keep your tongue from evil; depart from evil and do good" (Psalm 34:13–15). It is for the same reason that Moses addressed a warning to Israel, saying to them, "This shall be the law of the *metzora* [leper]," that is, the law relating to one that gives currency to an evil report.

(Leviticus Rabbah 16:2)

The choice of the psalm verse is poignant. "Who desires life?" (Psalm 34:13). Everyone desires life. Everyone would be a likely customer for this peddler, even the rabbi. An "elixir" is a cure-all. It's a word often associated with snake-oil salesmen of the past. Although the word "elixir" carries a negative connotation, an elixir is also something that is easy to swallow and makes us feel better. The elixir, of course, is nothing but Torah itself. Though the verse comes from Psalms, to the Rabbis it represents all Torah because it teaches us about God's ways.

The answer to the question is found not in a distant text or far-flung source, but rather in what follows immediately in Psalms: "Keep your tongue from evil; depart from evil and do good" (Psalm 34:14–15). It sounds like a sweet elixir by any standard; nevertheless, it is a challenge to those who can't keep themselves from an evil tongue, or *lashon ha'ra* in Hebrew, commonly understood as hearsay and rumors. In other words, it's yesterday's yenta and today's gossip.

The Rabbis proved their point when they parsed the word *metzora*. They taught that the word could be understood this way: *motzi [shem] ra*. *Motzi* means "to bring forth," as in the familiar blessing over the bread, *hamotzi lechem min ha'aretz*. *Ra* means "evil." *Shem* means "the Divine Name. Therefore, the *metzora* is certainly not only a physical leper, or whatever *metzora* might really mean; it is also one who "brings forth an evil report." The worst evil was nothing less than gossip, hearsay, and slander. The whole Torah could be destroyed by *lashon ha'ra*, "the evil tongue."

Evidence of this fact is observed in how the Jewish community responded to the AIDS crisis when it first appeared in the 1980s and then became part of our world in the 1990s. Some religious leaders condemned gays for the "sin" they committed and the punishment of HIV, which "they brought on themselves." They cited the same verses from Leviticus, only they used them as proof of the "leprosy that God visited on them." Their horrific conclusions raised the ire of moderate voices and religious leaders. Foremost were Jewish and moderate Christian voices, who used the same verses from Leviticus to point to the real lepers among us.

The midrash demonstrated that the real lepers among us were not the ones who were afflicted. Rather, the ones who gave "currency to an evil report" were the real lepers. Their hateful language, fear-mongering, and slander perpetrated the greatest evil when it tore apart families, congregations, and communities. In response, many synagogues and churches in communities around the country organized teams that befriended patients living with

AIDS whose own families and congregations had disowned them. They were mostly alone except for the few close friends and teams that helped them to seek basic needs, like food, medicine, and friendship. To those of us who participated in giving care and friendship, these men and women living with AIDS were not lepers who needed to be segregated because they were living with a ruthless disease. They were at the mercy of everyone around them. They were afflicted with a disease that confounded the scientific community and every thoughtful and concerned individual. When patients living with AIDS died, the team that provided friendship and care often attended the funerals. They were there in place of families who couldn't bring themselves to acknowledge the death, let alone the life, of their loved one.

The teenage son of an AIDS team member accompanied his mother on some visits to her client's home. During these visits, her son participated in conversations about daily needs and general subjects with the client. He acknowledged that his experience with the client revealed a simple but overarching truth that we're all human beings who can know joy and misery. The brief visits exposed the teenager not to disease, but to humanity. The mother was cautioned by her friends not to expose her son to a patient living with AIDS. She prepared her son for the visit and was amply rewarded by her son's own observations about life, personal choices, and unconditional love.

Adolescents can be critical of their peers, but they are also uniquely open to new ways to see the world and its inhabitants. Animals and people alike, especially vulnerable ones, can be recipients of teenagers' unique brand of openness and love. It should be accounted to them as a reflection of God's love for all God's creatures. It can be a quality that is nurtured in them so that it takes root and flourishes for a lifetime.

God's love for the people Israel, reflected in the covenant God made with Abraham, Isaac, and Jacob, Sarah, Rebecca, Rachel, and Leah, endures. The Torah and midrash take us to the place and time where one of the greatest challenges to the covenant was experienced at Mount Sinai. When the community struggles with challenges to its holiness and blessings, we remember that God's love is unconditional. And, when we see ourselves in the same place but in our own time, we learn for ourselves that just as God's covenant is eternal, so is God's love.

3

God Lives with Me

"Go forth from your native land and from your father's house to the land that I will show you."
—Genesis 12:1

God rewarded Abraham for every step he took.
—Genesis Rabbah 39:9

In Judaism, faith in God can be understood as the belief that God lives with us in all the times of our life. It's difficult to have perfect faith all at once. In adolescence and early adulthood, when we're likely to begin the large task of making our own choices, we want to believe that we can do it on our own. Without our parents to supervise us, we embark on our way. We pack up our college diploma or our street smarts, and we set out to make a name for ourselves. We believe in ourselves and so we ask others to believe in us, too. Along the way, we find eager supporters but just as many doubters. If we're honest with ourselves, we doubt ourselves sometimes, too. The inevitable fork in the road causes the most introspective among us to look for guidance on our way to a destination we can only imagine. At one time or another, all of us yearn for greater faith that the path we're on is the one intended for us. Such faith is bound up in our belief that God lives with us every day. In this chapter, we will explore ways to incorporate God's presence into our everyday lives in our years of early adulthood and independence.

Abraham's Journey

One of the greatest biblical stories is about Abraham (Abram). In the last few verses of Genesis 11, we learn first about Abraham's father, Terah, who brought his family to Haran:

> Terah took his son Abram, his grandson Lot the son of Haran, and his daughter-in-law Sarai, the wife of his son Abram, and they set out together from Ur of the Chaldeans for the land of Canaan; but when they had come as far as Haran, they settled there. The days of Terah came to 205 years; and Terah died in Haran.
>
> (Genesis 11:31–32)

Between the time Terah and his family lived in Haran and Abraham departed from there (Genesis 12), Torah is silent. The Rabbis' midrash explains what happened in Terah's house in Haran leading up to Abraham's journey from his father's house. Found in midrash and not in Torah, the story of Abraham smashing his father's idols is as famous for Jewish children as any children's fable:

> Rabbi Hiyya said: Terah was a manufacturer of idols. He once went away somewhere and left Abraham to sell them in his place. A man came and wished to buy one. "How old are you?" Abraham asked him. "Fifty years," was the reply. "Woe to such a man!" he exclaimed. "You are fifty years old and would worship a day-old

object!" At this he became ashamed and departed. On another occasion a woman came with a plateful of flour and requested him, "Take this and offer it to them." So he took a stick, broke them, and put the stick in the hand of the largest. When his father returned he demanded, "What have you done to them?" "I cannot hide it from you," he began to explain. "A woman came with a plateful of fine meal and requested me to offer it to them. One claimed, 'I must eat first,' while another claimed, 'I must eat first.' Thereupon the largest arose, took the stick, and broke them." "Why do you make fun of me?" he cried out. "Have the idols any knowledge!?" "Should not your ears listen to what your mouth is saying?" Abraham retorted.

(Genesis Rabbah 38:13)

A young Abraham reasoned that the clay figures his father fashioned could not possibly be gods who had also fashioned him and his father. It didn't make any sense to him. He could not perpetrate such pagan and false ideas on himself or others. His growth as a human being began in that place where he cast off his childhood images of clay gods. Likewise, we inherited from our parents images of God that served as precursors to our own. In childhood, we listened to and repeated after our parents, who modeled for us how to worship, how to believe, and how to bring God into our lives. They branded us with what had been familiar, consistent, and authentic images of God for many years.

When we passed through adolescence, we left much of our parents' homes behind us, too. Like Abraham, we left our parents' home to learn more about the world and to learn more about God for ourselves. In Genesis 12, God commanded Abraham to leave

behind everything he ever knew for a place God had not yet identified for him:

> The Lord said to Abram, "Go forth from your native
> land and from your father's house to the land that I will
> show you."
>
> (Genesis 12:1)

What's more, God sweetened Abraham's expectations. When he
arrived there by means of faith and fortitude, God would reward
him with a new name (Abraham) and a great destiny:

> "I will make of you a great nation,
> And I will bless you;
> I will make your name great,
> And you shall be a blessing.
> I will bless those who bless you
> And curse him that curses you;
> And all the families of the earth
> Shall bless themselves by you."
>
> (Genesis 12:2–3)

According to the Rabbis' midrash, Abraham left his father's
house, his father's idols, and every possession, custom, ritual,
and emotional attachment he had to his father's home. He left it
all behind in favor of a more lasting and real experience with
One God, beginning a journey to a place God had not yet shown
him. The difficulty in the Torah text is God's command to
Abraham to leave everything behind for a place he didn't know.
Without an explanation, the midrash wants to know, "Why did-
n't God show Abraham the place to which he was going, immediately?" The answer provides us ways to understand how God
lives with us at every turn and with every step we take in our

effort to reach our intended destination. So the Rabbis ask and answer:

> Why didn't God reveal the land to Abraham there and then? In order to make it more beloved in his eyes and to reward him for every step he took.
>
> (Genesis Rabbah 39:9)

The Rabbis asked the question because they anticipated our need to know whether faith in God was synonymous with blind loyalty. And if faith was, in fact, just blind loyalty, at what cost should it come to us? And, finally, if there are costs, what are the benefits?

This biblical event was about much more than God's will over Abraham. It was also about God's place in Abraham's everyday life. The Rabbis taught that God didn't show Abraham the place to which he was going immediately for two reasons: first, in order to make the place more beloved in Abraham's eyes; and second, to reward Abraham for each step he took in the right direction.

Abraham was young. He had just left his father's house, and this time it was permanent. How could God make the place to which he was going more beloved to Abraham than his childhood home? God made it possible for Abraham to desire the place in graduated steps as he drew closer to it. Immediate gratification was the way of his past. Like a young and impatient person, Abraham used to demand what he wanted, for he was as impetuous as he was faithful. In his effort to demonstrate that idols were nothing but clay figurines, Abraham destroyed his father's gods and made it appear that the largest idol destroyed the smaller ones. Abraham was immature, to be sure, but he certainly made his point. Abraham's departure from his father's house would not be impetuous. It would be guided and regulated. It would demand patience and obedience. Furthermore, the way of life Abraham led as a child of his father permitted fits of immaturity, but the life he entered when he followed the path led by God would have to be lived under more adultlike terms.

Walking with God

The Rabbis also taught that God was not only a guide for Abraham's journey; God also experienced each step along with him. God didn't show Abraham the place immediately so that God could bless him for each step he took. Every time Abraham moved in a positive direction, he was rewarded; thus, he continued to move along the straight path until finally he moved naturally in the right direction on his own. Yet Abraham did not move in the direction God was sending him only because he sought the reward that came with each step. Rather, Abraham took each step because he was confident that God's presence supported him. God and Abraham wanted the same things. God's own blessing was found in the richness of Abraham's life.

The same could be said of us. Certainly our childhood images of our parents were filled with some fond memories and fits of immaturity, too. They were days that allowed us some room to grow and test our limits, even when we were restricted by our parents' permission. When we left home for college or professional life, like Abraham, there was more freedom, but it wasn't unrestricted. Now, the way was outlined by boundaries drawn by employers, landlords, professors, and other authority figures, and navigating that path required patience and obedience. Without parents, faith in our ability to make our way became the difference between reaching our destination successfully or not.

Like Abraham, we embarked on new paths because we were fairly sure that the rewards we anticipated would be there for us.

We needed to make good choices and take the right steps. In Abraham's case, God promised him from the outset that he would be blessed and that all nations would be blessed through his name if he walked the path God outlined for him. Under those conditions, who wouldn't go? Our path is filled with less certain rewards, to be sure, but it still holds much potential.

Our society and culture maintain that if we earn an education, especially a university education, then we will be able to reap the rewards commensurate with such an achievement. Additionally, the rewards will be even greater if the individual also possesses unique talents. With some motivation, self-initiative, and energy, a person who is so inclined can, like Abraham, make a name for himself or herself and be remembered as a person of great achievements.

As we continue to see ourselves as descendants of Abraham, and as ones with whom God also lives, we cannot help but look for signs of our own success. But, like Abraham, we must take each step of our journey with extraordinary faith, because we never know when we will have reached the destination. There are people who skip steps and believe they still deserve every blessing. About such people, we might say that they were born on third base and believe they hit a triple. No doubt, those who were born on third base were born into privilege. They have what they need and probably never worry about what the future will hold, especially financially. But they also make gross assumptions about their own contribution to the place they came to hold so quickly in life.

There is no substitute for experience. Those who really hit the triple know the feelings of warming up, practicing for excellence at the plate, and rounding the corner to slide into third. And let's not forget all the lessons learned from previous attempts—hitting a fly ball that was caught in the outfield or striking out after three swings at the plate.

While there is no straight line between two points on our life's journey, and new junctures can be fraught with tumult, we learn from the midrash that God blessed Abraham for each step he took in the direction God set out for him. Psychologists might call this "behavior modification." Every time Abraham moved in a positive direction, he was rewarded; thus, he continued to move along the straight path until finally he moved naturally in the right direction on his own. The lesson is not lost on us either.

The motivation we need to accomplish our tasks is no less a function of God's presence in our lives than it was for Abraham. To participate in the covenantal relationship Abraham enjoyed with God, we have to recognize the strengths we have and the talents we possess and use them to bring honor to ourselves, to our families, and to God. When we identify work and a lifestyle that promote self, family, community, and God, then we can be more sure of our choice and the direction of our life. The behavior we adopt in our effort to achieve these tasks is derived from the knowledge we inherited from our religious tradition, the one our parents bequeathed to us. Even if they left our religious inheritance in tatters, it isn't without hope that we should pick it up again for ourselves.

Choosing Our Own Path

Remember that Abraham did not move in the direction God was sending him only because he sought the reward that came after each step. Rather, Abraham took each step because he was confident that God's presence supported him. Even when he faltered or stumbled, God didn't abandon him. God wanted Abraham to enjoy the richness of life found in the family he built with Sarah and in the faith he found in One God. Similarly, we should not choose our path only because we are confident that we will be rewarded. Rather, we should choose our path because we believe it will bring us meaning in our lives along the way. We can also know that God in Judaism joins us along the way to inspire us and bless us. Even after we stumble and pick ourselves up again, our faith is strengthened. After all, there is no such thing as a perfect life, but we can recognize that our lives have been blessed along the way.

Abraham's journey was three days long. He didn't know where he was going, and neither do we. The book of Genesis does not tell us that Abraham enjoyed the journey, that he rested along the way, or that he fought off bandits during the night. The Torah only tells us that he reached the end of his journey with God's blessing. Should we expect anything less or more?

Elie Wiesel wrote, "Being Jewish is not the pursuit of happiness; it is the pursuit of meaning." If we seek only happiness, then we will be disappointed from time to time. If we seek meaning, then we may discover that life and all its ambiguities are reflected in a variety of experiences that can also be sources of happiness.

One way to understand it is to compare our life experience to a roller coaster. As the roller coaster takes off, there is great anticipation because we have heard about what lies around the corner for us. Our anxiety rises with mounting anticipation of a hill of opportunity and potential energy. We scream with horror when we plunge into valleys that seem to consume us without any sign of escape. We approach a sharp turn, momentarily forgetting the past. We rush into new experiences we have no choice but to face. Finally, we catch our breath on level track, and when the car glides to a rest and we depart from it, pale with fear but with blood pumping from the exhilaration of it all, we are sure that we would like to take the ride again. Why? Because this time, we might even do it with our eyes open and our hands waving in the air. That's real life.

The meaning we find on our journey depends on what we choose to feel when we are climbing new heights, descending into the valleys, or leveling off. It is true that happiness can be found along the way, but we shouldn't expect it to permeate the experience. How can plummeting into the unknown not include some terror? How can the rise of new opportunities only be exciting? How can the end of the ride not be filled with thoughts of going around again?

At whatever stage in life we find ourselves, we are better prepared for life when we find meaning in the purpose of climbing, in the tendency to fall, and in the renewal of leveling off. Out of such meaning we may even find happiness. One goal, then, is to enrich each twist and turn with faith that God lives with us there, in that step and in that moment.

Another goal is to cling to faith that God lives with us, even when the roller coaster jumps the tracks and it never reaches its destination. Tragedy happens and our life takes unexpected spills we cannot begin to imagine or understand. In the book *The Spirituality of Imperfection*, Ernest Kurtz writes about how he suffered with the pain of addiction, which sidetracked his life until he came to new understandings. He cites a member of Alcoholics Anonymous who wrote, "Religion is for people who are afraid of going to hell; spirituality is for those who have been there."[1] His observation is stark. He believes that spirituality is a path that opens to us only after we have faced our human situation squarely. To be spiritual, then, is to be incredibly human. It means we can be in touch with our imperfections and our vulnerabilities and live with them. We can reach outward farther toward God when we become more aware of our humanness and revel in it.

Religion alone is not enough. Religion without spirituality is just a defense, a suit of armor against internal or external forces that might destroy us. Spirituality, on the other hand, is about living with our circumstances, whatever they might be. Spirituality reduces our impulse to remove stubborn or temporary problems and urges us to work with them instead. Sometimes, a stubborn problem requires nothing more than accepting what is inevitably true about ourselves, which is another way of saying that there are some truths that we cannot deny.

In the mishnah *Pirkei Avot*, also known as "Ethics of Our Fathers," our Sages asked, "Who is truly rich? He who is satisfied with his lot in life" (*Pirkei Avot* 4:1). We are born with all that we are going to have in the way of intellect, strength, and talents. We know it's coded in our DNA, and it's a product of our environment. We can choose what we will do with what we have been given, but we cannot always change what we have. Those who are satisfied are not complacent; rather, they are at peace with their circumstances and make the best of them.

Rabbi Samuel Karff, rabbi emeritus at Congregation Beth Israel, Houston, Texas, taught, "We are all spiritual people. The practice of one's own religion is the deepest expression of one's unique spirituality." Kurtz came to the same conclusion through his own life experiences with addiction. He discovered that he was a spiritual person, but he did not use religion to condemn his addiction or himself; rather, he saw his life's journey as a spiritual experience that led him to a destination he was intended to reach. Religion would never again be the end, but only the means. It was an honest place filled with more promise than he had ever known, and also with greater reward.

We should be so lucky to arrive at our destination as blessed as Abraham was. And, yet, our steps are no less important. Taken carefully and thoughtfully, our steps can reflect our best decisions and strongest hope that wherever we intend to go, God will be with us there. Even when we misstep, and we do, the wisdom to turn around or to find another way is a sign that God's presence is with us there, too, as a source of courage and inspiration. Ultimately, wherever we go can be a place that is filled with our trust that God lives with us.

4

God Teaches Me

*The Lord came down to look at the city
and tower that man had built.*
—Genesis 11:5–9

*God did not pass judgment or come to a conclusion
until God saw firsthand.*
—Midrash Tanchuma, Noach 18

Honoring Our Parents

God is everywhere and God loves us. Our Rabbis demonstrated these principles in midrash about God's omnipresence and unconditional love for us. They are two images of God that lead us to believe, from an early age, that wherever we go, God is there and so is God's compassion. As we grow older and make our way from our parents' house for the first time, we are obligated to do more than just receive God's love, for doing so would make us like babies who rely on their parents to give them everything they need. Even at a young age, children learn how to give back to others with gestures as small as a show of affection or with genuine expressions of selfless giving, like when a child makes a birthday card for a parent or a small gift for a grandparent or friend.

Children whose relationships with their parents don't include selfless acts have more trouble moving beyond childhood wants and needs. Adult children who do have mature relationships with their parents, on the other hand, can show love for their parents and others with more than rote expressions and physical signs of affection. They show love for their parents and others by honoring them. Good grades, good choices, self-sufficiency, and independence all bring honor to parents. Such demonstrations of maturity also bring parents *nachas*, real joy.

The Fifth Commandment says, "Honor your father and your mother, that you may long endure on the land that the Lord your God is giving you" (Exodus 20:12). "Honor" comes from the Hebrew word *kabeid*. It means honor, but it also means to give weight, consideration, and respect to the object of one's honor. It does not mean that children have to do whatever their parents tell them. At this point along our journey and away from home, honoring our parents by doing only what they tell us to do would impair us from reaching our intended destination on our own life's path. Therefore, the commandment isn't about obeying. The commandment is about respecting, listening to, and learning from our parents, even when we set aside their advice for more personal preferences.

Another critical insight into the Fifth Commandment is found in what it does not command. Nowhere in the Torah, including the Ten Commandments, are we commanded to *love* our parents. It sounds strange, but it's true. Love for our parents can be a by-product of a relationship in which parents and children respect one another and honor each other, but love cannot be commanded between them. Torah does, however, command us to love God.

Loving and Learning from God

The commandment to love God is highlighted in the words that follow the "watchword of our faith" in Torah. The *Shema* commands us, "Hear, O Israel! The Lord is our God, the Lord is One" (Deuteronomy 6:4). It continues:

> You shall love the Lord your God with all your heart and with all your soul and with all your might. Take to heart these instructions with which I charge you this day. Impress them upon your children. Recite them when you stay at home and when you are away, when you lie down and when you get up. Bind them as a sign on your hand and let them serve as a symbol on your forehead; inscribe them on the doorposts of your house and on your gates.
>
> (Deuteronomy 6:5–9)

We have a duty to return God's love. The *Shema* makes it clear how to show our love for God. We have to take Torah teachings to heart. That is, we have to write them, so to speak, on our hearts so that we will never forget them. Then, we can "recite them at home and when [we] are away, when [we] lie down and when [we] get up" (Deuteronomy 6:7). We are asked to reach a state of constant awareness of God—a state in which God's place in our lives and our love for God will be real to us all day and every day. Loving God, therefore, is not about praise alone. It is all about doing what God has commanded us to do.

The challenge goes beyond figuring out what the commandments are and how to do them. We have to make personal choices about which commandments are meaningful to us in our spiritual lives today. That might mean the difference between identifying with Reform, Conservative, or Orthodox Judaism or finding an alternative to the three major Jewish movements. But, to our purpose, affiliation with any one or more movements cannot be possible until and unless we learn how to do what we are obligated to do in a world where God's presence and God's love abound. To be good learners, we need a good teacher. Far from religious school teachers of the past or parents from our childhood, we need to embrace the Teacher-of-all-teachers who will be present to us all our life.

God is our master teacher. At the point at which we depart from our parents' home, we need to assemble lessons to take with us. Most likely, the first time we leave home is for college. We load the car with all our worldly goods and make our way to campus. But on our shoulders we might also take the lessons that our parents taught us. We do it stubbornly, but we know we can't leave without their insights. We also leave with the high expectations of finding our own insights and leading our lives according to our own outlook. It is now when we need God, in addition to teachers and professors, to be our mentor, a real master teacher.

More than belief for belief's sake, envisioning God as teacher enables us to learn from wisdom when we need it. At times when we're truly on our own, or choose to be, without our parents' opinions and decisions, we want to draw on a source of truth that is relevant and reliable. It's not in our interest to make mistakes; it's in our interest to do it on our own and to prove to ourselves and others that we can succeed. Searching for our own truth is the privilege of every young adult, and sometimes, in small ways, it's a fruitful process. More often, over time, familiar truths return to guide us on familiar paths. When we're ready, we find that those truths come from Torah, where God's master lessons have inspired many generations, including our own.

Becoming a Master Learner

Torah is full of examples of God's role as a master teacher and ours as master learners. One of the first examples of God as our teacher is found in Genesis, at the end of the portion called Noach. After the familiar story about Noah and the ark, we read the story of the Tower of Babel. It's there, in the Valley of Shinar, that God demonstrates a human lesson and God serves us by teaching us. There we find the people of the earth building a tower to heaven:

> Everyone on earth had the same language and the same words. And as they migrated from the east, they came upon a valley in the land of Shinar and settled there. They said to one another, "Come, let us make bricks and burn them hard."—Brick served them as stone, and bitumen served them as mortar.—And they said, "Come, let us build us a city, and a tower with its top in the sky, to make a name for ourselves; else we shall be scattered all over the world." The Lord came down to look at the city and tower that man had built, and the Lord said, "If, as one people with one language for all, this is how they have begun to act, then nothing that they may propose to do will be out of their reach."
>
> (Genesis 11:1–6)

As long as God held dominion over the entire earth, the people acting together believed that they were insufficiently prepared to take control of their part of the world or whatever part was left to them. So they began to build a tower to the heavens "to make a name for [them]selves." In effect, they were prepared to do battle with God. What happened next was a result of their communal demonstration of mistrust and lack of faith. They conspired against God, by using their common language and interests to build a tower and take control. Next, God responded:

> "Let us, then, go down and confound their speech there, so that they shall not understand one another's speech." Thus the Lord scattered them from there over the face of the whole earth; and they stopped building the city. That is why it was called Babel, because there the Lord confounded the speech of the whole earth; and from there the Lord scattered them over the face of the whole earth.
>
> (Genesis 11:7–9)

This small story tells much about God's personal interest in us and the lengths to which God goes to teach us. Remember that our Rabbis taught us that God is omnipresent and omniscient. God is everywhere, so God doesn't have to "come down" to see anything. God already sees. And God knows the answer to the problems on earth, because God is omniscient. So, the story raises a critical question, which the Rabbis address in a midrash. The question is, "Why did God, who is omnipresent and omniscient, have to come down to earth before passing judgment on the people?" The answer is given succinctly by the Rabbis:

> It is only to teach God's creations that God did not pass judgment or come to a conclusion until God saw firsthand.
>
> (*Midrash Tanchuma*, *Noach* 8)

In this midrash, the Rabbis demonstrate that one of the otherwise unseen roles God plays is that of teacher. God is a master teacher whose benevolence is shown by giving us the right way to go. Another reason the Rabbis create this role of God as teacher is to dissuade us, who might otherwise be doubtful of God's presence, from concluding that God is only up in heaven, and not everywhere as the Rabbis also taught us. If God were only up in heaven, then it would not be difficult to explain why Torah reports that God came down to earth. By interpreting God's coming down as a lesson for human creations, we are treated to more insights into God's compassion, love, and devotion for us.

The Rabbis also presumed that God knew what the people were doing and that they understood the consequences they faced. But God came down, as it were, to see for God's self and to judge the people based on hard evidence. Therefore, God's example teaches us how far we must go before we judge others. Only hard evidence and eyewitness testimony, not gossip or hearsay, will lead us to the most just conclusions.

At the end of the story of the Tower of Babel, the people were spread out to the four corners of the earth and their language was confounded. Now, if people set out to build a tower in order to do battle with God, their project would fail. If someone asked for a brick, his request would go unanswered because his words would not be understood; an order for pitch or bitumen would also go unfilled. Therefore, the place was aptly named. Today, the word "babble" still refers to speech that is unintelligible to everyone except maybe the one who is babbling.

God as teacher is vital to our renewed image of God. Rather than the old man who sat on a throne to teach us, this image of God's benevolence reassures us that God, like our favorite teachers, can mentor us in perpetuity. Though God's judgment at the Tower of Babel was severe, the means by which God came to judge is a time-honored lesson for all humanity.

Setting Out on Our Own

Though we feel ready to step out of our parents' home and out from under their authority when it's time to choose our own place to live and our own career, we still want some assurances that we are not always alone. Somehow we can't let go of the safety nets our parents provided us for so many years. The credit card in their name covers emergency bills or some small conveniences they agreed to pay. The health insurance they provide makes it possible to work part-time jobs and carry a full load of classes at the same time. Even the old family car they pass on to us makes life a little easier. It isn't unusual for young adults to postpone their independence in favor of a little more time on their parents' dole. It feels good, because it's easier, but it's no way to grow up and find the independence they really crave. Eventually, we must all transition into independent adulthood.

There is a precedent for this transition. It's modeled in Torah, where Moses was almost ready to lead the Israelites away from Mount Sinai, to continue their journey to the Promised Land. There, Moses paused to turn to God and ask for more than God's presence along the way. Moses wanted a surety, a safety net, too. It happened after the incident of the Golden Calf, when the people who participated in the sinful act died from plague:

> Then the Lord said to Moses, "Set out from here, you and the people that you have brought up from the land of Egypt, to the land of which I swore to Abraham, Isaac, and Jacob."
>
> (Exodus 33:1)

After all that he had experienced, Moses was not satisfied that he could "set out from here" and lead the people on his own. He needed more. He needed a surety just like any young leader who hasn't been fully "battle tested" yet. Despite Moses's plea, like a child wanting more, God provided only what God could give and only what Moses needed:

> Moses said to the Lord, "See, You say to me, 'Lead this people forward,' but You have not made known to me whom You will send with me. Further, You have said, 'I have singled you out by name, and you have, indeed, gained My favor.' Now, if I have truly gained Your favor, pray let me know Your ways, that I may know You and continue in Your favor."
>
> (Exodus 33:12–13)

If that were not enough, Moses went for broke. He reminded God of the previous conversation they shared when the people were caught worshiping the Golden Calf. Moses said, "Consider, too, that this nation is *Your* people" (Exodus 33:13). God acquiesced and said to Moses, "I will also do this thing that you have asked; for you have truly gained My favor and I have singled you out by name" (Exodus 33:17).

Here, now, Moses relied heavily on the special status he earned as God's faithful servant. Moses's greatness was only as good as God's presence, but there was a limit:

> [Moses said to God,] "Oh, let me behold Your Presence!" And [God] answered, "I will make all My goodness pass before you, and I will proclaim before you the name Lord, and the grace that I grant and the compassion that I show. But," [God] said, "you cannot see My face, for man may not see Me and live." And the Lord said, "See there is a place near Me. Station yourself

on the rock and, as My Presence passes by, I will put you
in a cleft of the rock and shield you with My hand until
I have passed by. Then I will take My hand away and you
will see My back; but My face must not be seen."

(Exodus 33:18–23)

In God's response to Moses, God demonstrated remarkable compassion between Creator and creation, between God and servant.
We should be moved by the willingness God showed Moses to be
present for him as a guide and teacher, without any threat or risk
to his well-being. The courtesy God showed Moses by placing him
in the cleft of the rock and showing him God's back prepared
Moses to go the way he was intended to go into the wilderness and
into the years that would define his life and his legacy.

Better than a single sighting of God, from which Moses
would not have survived, God demonstrated once more God's
commitment to our ancestors, Abraham, Isaac, and Jacob, to Moses,
and to us. God essentially said to Moses, "I will show you My
ways." These are the teachings upon which Moses would rely.
These are also the teachings upon which our lives are built.

As it was for Moses, when we too are on our own for the first
time, God, as teacher, helps us along our way. A new apartment
in a new city, a new job with a new boss, new bills and obligations, and new expectations that our hard work will fulfill all our
hopes and dreams—these are just a few ways we step out of a
world that was familiar into a world that is just coming into view.
It cannot happen in a vacuum. However we define success, it cannot happen without many resources to support us. We need good
relationships with neighbors, coworkers and colleagues, bankers,
business people, family, and friends. We need to learn from them
and live with them, even when we have to work around them.

There is no better time to have God on our side as teacher, guide, and mentor than when we leave the security and safety nets of institutions of higher learning and our parents' homes.

Reaching for Success

One of our first major life goals is simply to succeed, be it in our field of study, in a profession, or in a major interest. Our ancestors traversed many lands to realize their dreams in a Promised Land. Our hope to realize our dreams is not any different. Unlike the people at the Tower of Babel, our goal, like that of our ancestors, is to reach success *with* God, not *against* God.

Our Judaism assures us that success is what we should aim to achieve. But Judaism does not value success as highly as it values how that success was achieved. There is no guarantee that it will be easy, but Judaism is clear about how it can be earned. Torah is honest about life's opportunities and challenges:

> See, I set before you this day life and prosperity, death and adversity. For I command you this day, to love the Lord your God, to walk in [God's] ways, and to keep [God's] commandments, [God's] laws, [God's] rules, that you may thrive and increase, and that the Lord your God may bless you in the land that you are about to enter and possess.
>
> (Deuteronomy 30:15–16)

"To walk in God's ways" is a repetition of the promise God made to Moses, an assurance that God is his teacher and ours. We learn from God and we honor God by walking in God's ways, keeping God's commandments, laws, and rules. The expectation is that when we do these things we will know some measure of success. The alternative seems obvious, but if we hear it only in biblical terms, we might be terribly discouraged and disbelieving. The opposite of the blessing we might receive by walking in God's ways is the curse we might receive by rejecting God's teachings.

> But if your heart turns away and you give no heed, and are lured into the worship and service of other gods, I declare to you this day that you shall certainly perish.
>   (Deuteronomy 30:17–18)

To our ancestors, the opposite of God's blessing was surely God's curse. From our contemporary perspective, we can think about a blessing as the dividend we make ourselves available to receive or feel when we learn from God and follow God's ways. We can think about a curse as the missed opportunity or the path we should have taken. Now we only see it in hindsight, but we can retrieve from it an important lesson learned.

For example, when we leave our parents' home to make our way in the world, we admit that a part of the umbilical cord is never truly cut. What do we do with it? While young adults are growing up and making their way, parents often fail to see themselves as adults who are still growing up, too. So, they insist on preserving the connection they used to enjoy when their children were young and at home. Part of their dependence on their children is due to the lack of depth in their personal relationships with a spouse or friends. So, they call often, and their adult children fall back into familiar roles and speak to their parents as often as they call.

But thoughtful young adults will honor their parents by setting boundaries. Reasonable parents don't want to intrude, but they don't want to be excluded either. A call from young adults to their parents at a regular time, such as every evening at six o'clock or every Sunday morning, increases calm and decreases anxiety in families. Parents love nothing more than to hear the phone ring at the same time for their prearranged call. By doing so, young adults and their parents find God's blessings for themselves in the time they now have to themselves and in the time they share with each other on mutual terms.

The opposite is not a curse, even if it feels that way. In truth, the opposite is only the absence of blessing. When we shut out the lesson that God gives us so that we can "walk in God's ways," we effectively shut out the opportunity for blessing. The humanity in God's lesson at the Tower of Babel is a remarkable expression of God's hope that we can learn from life and embrace opportunities to enrich it.

In general, success can be infatuating for young adults who get on the fast track in corporate life. A young man once told me about his business experiences. He was living well at a young age. It impressed everyone around him, and he was enjoying it. As he described his exceptional and early prosperity, and what I considered to be a proverbial Tower, I gently suggested that even in the midst of success he should be careful to recognize what physics teaches us—namely, what goes up must come down. Markets fluctuate. It's a basic law of economics even under the best conditions. Nonetheless, he was confident. He was also adamant that his optimistic viewpoint was consistent with the market and his future. It wasn't much later that his optimistic Tower showed some signs of biblical influence, and soon it all came crashing down in a heap of economic crises.

At the end of Deuteronomy 30, God spells it out succinctly for the Israelites:

> I have put before you life and death, blessing and curse.
> Choose life—if you and your offspring would live—by

loving the Lord your God, heeding [God's] commands,
and holding fast to [God].

(Deuteronomy 30:19–20)

What's more is that God's promise was not only for them but also
for all time. The merit of our ancestors still devolves on us in this
time of our life and for the rest of our years:

For thereby you shall have life and shall long endure
upon the soil that the Lord swore to your ancestors,
Abraham, Isaac, and Jacob, to give to them.

(Deuteronomy 30:20)

Since then, learning from God's ways has been integral to personal
human choice. The story of the Tower of Babel is about the negative consequences of one people who spoke one language. But it
can also tell a larger story about what people can achieve in general. In our life, God cares enough to teach us. God did not destroy
the people of Babel. God merely scattered them about the face of
the earth. Many of us do not live in the place where we were
born. We and our families are scattered, too. We are divided among
many places and separated by many miles. Our ancestors
depended on the promise that when they lived by God's teachings,
they would also live among God's blessings. It has been said,
"Grow where you are planted." As we go (grow) from place to
place with work and relationships, God's blessings are abundant
enough for those who seek them through God's teachings.

5

God Hears Me

*Anything blind, or injured, or maimed ... such you shall
not offer to the Lord.*

—Leviticus 22:22

*When he acted with special courtesy, the Holy One,
blessed be God, acted toward him with special courtesy.*

—Leviticus Rabbah 11:5

As students, we were tested on what we learned. A passing
grade meant that we could move on to the next level. A failing grade meant that we had to do it again or sometimes just take
our lumps. In adulthood, we are still tested at work and at home
with family. The challenges at work and home are far different
than any written exam on a particular subject. Now our challenges test our mettle in every category of our life. Meeting the
demands of marriage, children, or extended family, let alone
work and career, can make college seem like the easiest time of
our life. Different as they are, college exams and challenges at
home and work share one thing in common: our success or failure depends largely, if not squarely, on what we choose to bring
to both kinds of tests.

A full adult life is all about relationships. Whether we are married or single, our relationships with our family and friends depend on our ability to listen and to be heard. It isn't clear whether it is easier to communicate successfully with family or with friends. They both know our strengths and weaknesses, even our sensitive subjects and hot buttons. We hide certain subjects from them and reserve the most personal for those we believe are closest to us. But no matter how many relationships we enjoy as adults, we should not deny ourselves the intimacy that can be created between us and God.

We seek a relationship with God that assures us that God hears us. Torah teaches that God does hear our prayers and personal meditations. God hears us according to what we bring to God; likewise, what we bring is all that we can expect to get back from God. Our challenge is to find the right words and means of expression so that our offering will be acceptable. Like our ancestors, we might also tremble before God when we struggle to find the right words and the right place in our heart. To prepare ourselves, we need to lay claim to the places from which we offer our prayers—not just in the synagogue, but also in our homes and workplaces, as well as in our hearts and souls.

Addressing God through Sacrifice

As recorded in Leviticus, God told Moses about the animal sacrifices God would accept from the Israelite people. In the wilderness and much later in the Temple in Jerusalem, offerings were brought to God, to express thanksgiving, repentance, and so forth:

> The Lord spoke to Moses, saying: Speak to Aaron and
> his sons, and to all the Israelite people, and say to them:
> When any man of the house of Israel or of the strangers

in Israel presents a burnt offering as his offering for any
of the votive or any of the freewill offerings that they
offer to the Lord, it must, to be acceptable in your favor,
be a male without blemish, from cattle or sheep or
goats. You shall not offer any that has a defect, for it will
not be accepted in your favor.

(Leviticus 22:17–20)

The requirements for animal offerings were clear. In order to be
"acceptable," they had to be without any blemish. The definition
of a blemish was not left to interpretation. It was recorded in
Torah. The text continues:

Anything blind, or injured, or maimed, or with a wen
[cyst], boil-scar, or scurvy—such you shall not offer to
the Lord.

(Leviticus 22:22)

Torah describes categories of obvious blemishes that any keen eye
could detect under close scrutiny. The offering made to God was
expected to be perfect and "acceptable in God's favor." These high
standards might have led Jews in their time to believe that only if
their sacrifices were perfect were their relationships with God perfect and that imperfect sacrifices were reason enough to despair
over them. The Rabbis sought to correct such a misnomer in their
midrash, as we will see below.

In Temple times, offerings weren't always brought from
long distances. They were also purchased when the pilgrim
arrived at the Temple grounds. There he could exchange his
money for a worthy animal for offering. After taking a ritual
bath, he would collect his offering and make his way to the
Temple Mount. There he offered his animal to the priest for

sacrifice. Were there unscrupulous salesmen selling "blemished" goats like day-old bread? Surely there were, but Torah and Talmud mostly record the teachings and the laws that represented ideals and lawful practices surrounding animal sacrifice. Torah and Talmud do not record that a bearer of sacrifices was turned away.

Finally, the animal was offered in the condition in which it was received. It was duly inspected and turned over to the priest for a sacrifice appropriate to the purpose of the person who brought it. Then, as the following midrash makes clear, the offering was received by God in the manner in which it was given. What the pilgrim carried in his arms to the Temple Mount, whether from home or from the nearby stall, was only the physical offering. The Rabbis, sure to subordinate the role of the priests-of-old to themselves, taught that the role of the priest was truly secondary compared to the real relationship between God and the individual pilgrim.

They demonstrated their findings by relating verses from Psalm 18:26ff to Moses:

> Rabbi Nehemiah expounded the verse as referring to Moses. When he approached God with special courtesy, God treated him with special courtesy; when he came to God with frankness, God answered him with frankness; when he approached God with lack of directness, God countered him with lack of directness; when he sought a clear statement regarding his affairs, God made clear his affairs for him.
>
> (Leviticus Rabbah 11.5)

The midrash explains that Moses showed "special courtesy" to God when he said, "Oh, let me behold Your Presence!" In response, God decided to show Moses all God's glory (Exodus 33:18–19). Moses showed "frankness" when he said, "Why doesn't the bush burn up?" (Exodus 3:3). God answered, "My glory is present therein." Moses showed "lack of directness" when he said, "When they say to me, 'What is God's name?' what will I say to them?" God said, "This is My name for the time being: I am that I am" (Exodus 3:13–14). When Moses sought a "clear statement regarding his affairs," God said, "I will send you to Pharaoh, that you may bring My people out of Egypt" (Exodus 3:10, 4:23, 5:23, 6:1). Consistent with the Rabbis' teaching, God does not reject our offerings either; rather, God accepts our offerings as they are received.

Prayer: The Modern Sacrifice

Our offerings are no longer physical sacrifices. When the Temple in Jerusalem was destroyed by the Romans in 70 CE, sacrifices were no longer able to be brought to priests. The age of Rabbinic Judaism took hold, and sacrifices were replaced by prayers. Although the offerings changed form in substance, they did not change so much in purpose. God hears us, too. Our daily worship includes the prayer "Praised are You, Eternal our God, *shomei'a tefilah*, who hears prayer."

In Hebrew, the word for sacrifice is *korban*, from the Hebrew root that means "to come close" or "to draw near." When the pilgrims brought their animal sacrifices, they brought them close to God. Since then, we have brought our prayers close to God, and not to a priest or a rabbi. By definition, a rabbi is a teacher, not an intermediary. The relationship we have with God is personal and direct. When we bring our prayers to God, they act as intimate conversation between ourselves and God and become our primary means of developing our adult relationship with God.

One aspect of ancient sacrificial practice remains with us today: the importance of our intentions when we enter into prayer. Like the pilgrim who brought an offering without blemish, we should strive to bring our prayers without blemish, too. They are the best we can do, even when we cannot recite the Hebrew perfectly or at all. A classic Jewish folktale makes the point:

> The Baal Shem Tov was praying together with his students in a small Polish village. Through his spiritual vision, the Baal Shem Tov had detected that harsh heavenly judgments had been decreed against the Jewish people, and he and his students were trying with all the sincerity they could muster to cry out to God and implore God to rescind these decrees and grant the Jews a year of blessing. This deep feeling took hold of all the inhabitants of the village, and everyone opened his heart in deep prayer. Among the inhabitants of the village was a simple shepherd boy. He did not know how to read; indeed, he could barely say the letters of the *aleph-bet*, the Hebrew alphabet. As the intensity of feeling in the synagogue began to mount, he decided that he also wanted to pray. But he did not know how. He could not read the words of the prayer book or mimic the prayers of the other congregants. He opened the prayer book to the first page and began to recite the letters—*aleph, bet, gimmel*—reading the entire *aleph-bet*. He then called out to God, "This is all I can do. God, You know how the prayers should be pronounced. Please, arrange the letters in the proper way." This simple, genuine prayer resounded powerfully within the heavenly

court. God rescinded all the harsh decrees and granted the Jews blessing and good fortune.

(Adapted from a story by the Baal Shem Tov)

God hears our prayers, and as long as they are offered sincerely, they are acceptable to God. Prayers of the heart are considered to be our best offering, and in the absence of any fixed prayer, they are also worthy. What's more, while Hebrew is a "holy tongue" and the preferred language for prayer among observant Jews, more than 150 years ago liberal Judaism established that praying in one's native tongue (e.g., German, English) was an acceptable means to fulfilling our obligations in prayer.

Contemporary prayers take many forms. They can be literal or thematic translations of traditional liturgy. They can also be wordless chants. Through them we find ways to ask God for healing, clarity, abundance, peace, or other personal issues. We also give thanks to God or ask for God's help on behalf of someone else. Still, some of us may find it difficult to relate to prayer conceptually. Unless it produces what we seek, it's difficult to believe that it makes a difference. These are childhood expectations that cause us to resist what appear to be outdated images we may harbor of God.

A young couple, expecting their first child, once asked me for my counsel as they struggled with these very issues. The wife was being observed in the hospital during the last few days leading up to her delivery date. The couple spoke about their concerns and the options that lay before them as they faced the birth of their child. Before the conversation ended, I suggested that we should share a prayer. The husband's facial expression made it very clear that he was uncomfortable with the notion of prayer. He said that he was far from a believer, whatever that meant to him. I acknowledged his discomfort, although it probably grew out of nothing more than his lack of experience. I assured him that prayers need not be petitionary, but they could help him to seek God as a source of courage in this difficult time. I suggested that, like chicken soup, another unscientific Jewish therapy, it couldn't hurt. He agreed to try.

For the wife's sake we continued. We prayed for their courage and patience, and we prayed to God to guide the hands of the doctors who served them. And we prayed for peace between them. Finding a balance between faith and science, the parents felt "covered," as the husband put it. Sometime later, the baby was born healthy and strong. I can't tell you that the new father's faith in God was restored to wholeness, but I am fairly confident that his expectations of God in his family life might lead him to conclude for himself that prayer "couldn't hurt."

Standing before God has never been a light matter. It wasn't easy in the ancient Temple of Jerusalem, and it is still not easy for us today in our synagogue, at home, or in the hospital. Oftentimes, we have to prepare ourselves for our conversations with God. Like the young husband in the hospital, we might feel unclear or even untutored in the way of prayer. It's possible to begin again with the prayers we recite in the liturgy of the High Holy Days. They help us feel whole again and able to stand before God. On Rosh Hashanah and Yom Kippur, we say, "Teach us to forgive ourselves for all these sins, O forgiving God, and help us to overcome them." These words resonate within us because we are often the last ones to forgive ourselves. Even after we recite our litany of sins and God says, "I have pardoned in response to your plea," and even after our friends and family forgive us, we are slow to forgive ourselves, and more often than not we create stumbling blocks for ourselves. These stumbling blocks often take the form of lingering guilt for deeds that made us feel less than whole. Maybe we haven't prayed often enough. Maybe we forgot how to do it. Maybe we feel less than an authentic religious person. We find ourselves unfit to bring an offering to God, even in the form of a prayer from our heart. Despite God's love for us, we just don't know what to say. And we worry: if we don't get it right, is it really possible for God to hear us and to respond?

The good news is that it is never too late to develop a line of communication with God. There is room for error, and even more room for improvement. Once we can begin to overcome our self-made stumbling blocks, we can grow close to God and bring forth what we want God to hear from us.

Choosing Unblemished Words

We have read in the past, "To err is human." Indeed, making mistakes is normal and natural. Usually we learn from our mistakes and move on. Sometimes we need some help. We find help from sources like therapists and close friends. But healing also comes from sources inside us, like renewed self-esteem and budding self-respect. Remember, as we learn in morning services, we were created in God's image, and the soul that God implants within us is a pure soul. When we don't help ourselves up and over stumbling blocks, we diminish the creativity God instilled within us. We have to make the effort.

"To forgive divine," concludes the familiar quotation. We have come to believe that forgiveness is something only God can provide. God does provide forgiveness when we seek it, just as God responds courteously when we bring courtesy to God. But Judaism doesn't give God, alone, the privilege to grant some pardon. When we make apologies for our actions or explain our transgressions to those we have offended, we begin the process of helping others to forgive us. Next, we come to God seeking the same forgiveness. And yet, despite it all, we are still the ones who can't forgive ourselves completely. We linger in a self-made world cut off from all the blessings God wants us to enjoy when God lives with us along the way.

The Jewish poet Abraham ben Samuel Abulafia (thirteenth century) wrote:

> I have tested the hearts of those who hate me, but no one hates me as my own heart does. Many are the blows and wounds inflicted by my enemies, but no one batters me and wounds me as my soul does.... To whom can I cry out, whom can I condemn, when those who are destroying me come from within myself? I have found nothing better than to seek refuge in Your mercy ... God who sits upon the Throne of mercy!"[2]

When we truly despair and see nothing of value within us, the poet writes, we have to look to God. The message on the High Holy Days is that we cannot despair. Who taught us that we had to be perfect, anyway? Our parents? Our teachers? Were they perfect? Our task is not to err so that we may be forgiven. Our task is to do the best we can and to know that when we miss the mark, and we will, we have the privilege to speak up and to be heard. Our friends and family do it. God does it, too.

The challenge for us will be how prepared we are to bring the offering we want to be received. Maybe it was easier in the past when our ancestors brought their animal sacrifices. They looked over the animal, found it free from blemishes, and gave it over to the priest to appease God and bring favor to their family. Even the aroma in the air sent the message that they had fulfilled their obligations. Today, the pressure is greater. We have to open our hearts to find the words to express our wants and needs. It isn't always easy, but it is our responsibility.

Every person in every generation has the same responsibility to choose words without blemish. That is not to say that everybody can be eloquent and articulate. Rather, from the most intimate to the most distant relationship, we have a duty to bring words that reflect who we are, what we need, and how we want to be received. The earliest lessons we learned came from our parents. They taught us to say "please" and "thank you." It was more than a lesson in respect and civics; it was the beginning of understanding how powerful our words can be. They are more than means to communication. They are also means to our sense of wholeness in our life. We learned early on that when we used the words our parents taught us successfully, we were rewarded. If we didn't understand the depth of their lesson then, it's important that we grasp it now.

The Importance of Shabbat

Our personal life is filled with opportunities to bring our own offerings to God in the form of prayers, shared rituals, and communal worship. The altar to which our ancestors brought their offerings was, in effect, not much different than the altar to which we bring our prayers. At home, the altar is the Sabbath table we set with a white tablecloth, beautiful candlesticks, silver *Kiddush* cup, and fancy challah plate. Now, the Sabbath table is ready for our rituals. There we recite the blessings for candles, wine, and challah, and we partake of them accordingly. With our family and friends around us or in our thoughts, our heads and hearts are attuned to the sanctity of the time and place that we create, together. While we can't tune out the noise of the busy streets around us, we do make our homes holy (set apart) spaces where our words of blessing can be heard by God.

A custom that many enjoy around the Sabbath table is the opportunity to interject personal words of gratitude for the joys and blessings of the past week. After all, the Sabbath is not a day to create or work; it is a day to rest and give thanks. A husband might share words of gratitude for his family and his wife. It wasn't long ago that husbands traditionally recited Proverbs 31:10–31, also known as "A Woman of Valor," on Shabbat, to highlight the role of the woman of the house. Although today many women are opposed to its gender-based message, its purpose is clearly to honor the woman of the house. Similarly, everybody at the table, including the children, can recite words of gratitude for everyone else.

Words at the Sabbath table easily become words we use in the synagogue. It is but a small leap from our home to the synagogue, where we open the prayer book to participate in a worshiping community. There with others, we sing and read our prayers to express gratitude, as well as wants and needs to God. Another small leap we can make is from the Sabbath table to private moments when we open up ourselves to offer to God the meditations of our hearts.

The habit we create through regular Shabbat ritual at home on Friday night and worship in the synagogue can lead us to value the power we possess to choose our words and offerings in every part of our life. Our desire to be heard by God is vital to our sense of wholeness. Our desire to be heard by our spouses, partners, children, and friends is also vital to our sense of well-being. The words we choose and how we convey them to God should be identical to the words we speak and how we convey them to the most important people in our lives.

Tefilat Halev: Prayer of the Heart

Like the boy who prayed using the letters of the Hebrew *aleph-bet*, we might not always choose our words perfectly. But we can dig deeper than ever before to give God our best effort. Genuine emotion, our Rabbis teach us, is more effective than poetic words or memorized prayers in any language. When Miriam and Aaron spoke against their brother, Moses, "because of the Cushite woman he had married" (Numbers 12:1), God punished them. Miriam was "stricken with snow-white scales" (Numbers 12:10). At first, Aaron pleaded on her behalf to Moses:

> "O my lord, account not to us the sin which we committed in our folly. Let her not be as one dead, who emerges from his mother's womb with half his flesh eaten away."
> (Numbers 12:11–12)

Then, in the simplest of words, Moses turned to God and prayed for his sister, "O God, pray heal her!" (Numbers 12:13). In Hebrew, the prayer is beautiful and alliterative: *El na, r'fa na lah!* The Hebrew is poetic but simple. It makes its point. The English, while terse, also teaches us that prayer is not always about poetry. Sometimes, it's about our gut reaction and direst needs. "Please God, heal her" is the shortest and most demanding prayer in Torah. It's remarkable in its brevity and its efficacy. Though Miriam was shut out of the camp for seven days to heal from her infirmity, the camp did not move on until Miriam returned to it safely and cleansed.

The ease with which we can come to prayer is a stunning invitation that comes to us in adulthood. Far from the pews where we recited prayers by rote for our teachers when we were young, we now find prayer is available to us in the pew, at home, in the hospital, and along the way. If we choose to use them, written prayers and services provide structure and focus that some may find comforting and helpful. They are welcome when we can recall them from memory and understand their purpose now, just as they were recited in the past. But they are not our sole source of prayers. Prayer of the heart, or "*tefilat halev*," are the prayers that grow out of our personal needs and our relationship with God. Sometimes, without knowing where else to turn, we utter what is in our hearts and souls. This is when, as it was for Moses, poetry is unnecessary and God hears our prayer.

In the words we are given and in the words of our hearts, God responds in kind to what we can offer. Especially now, when life is what we make of it, separated from our parents and childhood homes, God hears us as we want to be heard.

6

God Knows Me

You shall bring forward your brother Aaron, with his sons, from among the Israelites, to serve Me as priests.

—Exodus 28:1

God said to Moses, "I know that Aaron's intention was quite good."

—Exodus Rabbah 37:2

We are defined by our roles. We want to nurture and deepen them. Some of us are able to juggle multiple roles and succeed in most of them, but many of us struggle in this task and feel that we're coming up short most of the time. When we are many things to many people and wear many hats in many settings, we can feel like we are losing ground and not measuring up to anyone's expectations.

We run through our days to keep up with all the roles we are supposed to play. As parents, we give everything we can to our children. As employees and employers, we provide most of our energy to the "greater good" and the bottom line. The wants and needs of other people become our responsibility to satisfy. At the end of the day, as individuals, we get to keep for ourselves only whatever strength might remain. This is a challenging time in our life. After years of academic and other kinds of success, we begin to fail here and there. Our intentions were never better, but somehow we can't finish our tasks on time and our competition is gaining on us. The good news is, we don't have to lose face or lose ground. We just need to internalize that others can only measure our deeds; they cannot also know our intentions. A better balance at work and home can earn us more success, but even when we stumble it's important to preserve what we can still know about ourselves. We mean well. We want to achieve. We are not failures.

Our image of God helps us find peace when we recognize the difference between what others can know about us and what only God can know about us. It isn't easy to expose our deepest feelings to others when they seek to know everything about us. However, it should be increasingly comfortable to be in the presence of God, who knows our deeds and intentions. If not with God, then with whom? Because God loves us unconditionally, lives with us along the way, and hears us, it is important that God should know us, too. It is a place of comfort we arrive at after others have judged us for good or for ill. To feel in our hearts that God knows us can be the greatest measure of how well we are doing and how far we have yet to go.

There comes a time in our life when we look for standards by which to measure our deeds and sense of purpose. If we are just getting by but we feel like we're failing inside, we need an authentic way to measure what matters most so we can prioritize our roles and interests. Our goal is to be sincere about who we are and what we stand for.

In our most intimate relationships, we can struggle to succeed. Many demands leave us limited personal time. We have less of ourselves to devote to intimate conversations about love and life. Our friendships can suffer as we find ourselves spending more time at work and less time on the phone or across the table from those we hold dear. As a result, we miss out on the chance to commiserate about life's challenges and demands with our partners, friends, and relatives. Those encounters, though casual to us, provide standards by which we can measure how we're doing compared to others whom we admire and respect. Since we cannot do it all, as much as we try, and we cannot succeed perfectly everywhere and every time we apply ourselves, we have to rely on those who are dearest to us. They will be better than anyone else at understanding our intentions, especially when we fall short of their expectations.

Aaron and the Golden Calf

Our adult image of God needs to include our expectation that God can know us intimately. God's understanding of our intentions should give us comfort. God's acceptance of our best efforts can provide us the calm that we need in the midst of heavy demands on our personal and professional time. God's presence can help us feel secure even when others might misunderstand us. Our need to be understood by those dearest to us, especially when our intentions outweigh our deeds, is highlighted in the biblical story of Moses and Aaron at Mount Sinai. Evaluating our own success at home and in the world at large will depend on the lessons we can derive from these texts.

From the Torah text we have already explored in chapter 2 (Exodus 32), it appears that Aaron was complicit in the construction of the Golden Calf. This was a sin of extraordinary proportions, and its significance should not be underestimated. The Golden Calf undermined the very essence of the Israelites' redemption from Egypt. God said to the Israelites, "You shall be My people, and I shall be your God" (Exodus 6:7). The Rabbis explain this to mean that the Israelites will be a people by virtue of their covenant with God. What's more, God can only be God, as it were, if the Israelites will be God's people. They came out of Egypt in order to arrive at Mount Sinai, where God would give them Torah for all time. If this were derailed by the Israelite's pagan act of desecration and idol worship, then they would have no reason for being. Torah reports that those who were guilty in the sin of the Golden Calf were punished. God made the people account for their sins:

> The Lord said to Moses, "He who has sinned against Me, him only will I erase from My record. Go now, lead the people where I told you. See, My angel shall go before you. But, when I make an accounting, I will bring them to account for their sins." Then the Lord sent a plague upon the people, for what they did with the calf that Aaron made.
>
> (Exodus 32:33–35)

What about Aaron? Would Aaron be held to account for his sin, too? The Rabbis give us many different answers to this question. On the one hand, it's easy for them to make the case that Aaron was complicit and that he did commit a sin against God—after all, he gave them instructions and helped them fashion the idol himself. But a remarkable and contrary interpretation is made that exonerates Aaron. A close examination of the text reveals that Aaron was under immense pressure from the people. We know that the people "gathered against" Aaron. As he tried to serve Moses and God, and now the Israelite people, Aaron juggled as much as humanly possible in his hour of crisis. The Rabbis interpret Aaron's complicity not as a guilty act, but rather as a means of occupying the people while Moses was delayed on Mount Sinai.

When Moses saw with his own eyes what the people were doing and that his brother was at the center of it all, he was incensed. He smashed the tablets and pointed his finger of blame against everyone who participated in the sinful act. Torah doesn't record any words against Aaron, but his silence tells everything. When it was time for Aaron to step up and perform his duties as high priest, none other than Moses was commanded by God to bring him forward.

> You shall bring forward your brother Aaron, with his sons, from among the Israelites, to serve Me as priests: Aaron, Nadab and Abihu, Eleazar and Ithamar, the sons of Aaron. Make sacral vestments for your brother Aaron, for dignity and adornment. Next you shall instruct all who are skillful, whom I have endowed with the gift of skill, to make Aaron's vestments, for consecrating him to serve Me as priest.
>
> (Exodus 28:1–3)

But why did Aaron need to be brought up by his brother? Apart from courtesies and protocols, Aaron was fully capable of bringing himself forward. Aaron's role as high priest was not a mystery to Moses. He was fully aware of the tasks he was responsible for performing with the Israelites and on their behalf. Why, then, did God tell Moses to bring his brother, Aaron, forward?

The Rabbis provided an answer that reconciled what Aaron was doing with what Moses thought he was doing. It was the difference between Aaron's intentions and his deeds. Moses could know something about Aaron's deeds, but he could not know anything about his intentions. Only God knew Aaron's intentions.

On the verse "You shall bring forward your brother" (Exodus 28:1), the Rabbis commented:

> The Sages said: When Moses descended from Sinai and beheld Israel engaged in that unspeakable act, he looked at Aaron, who was beating the Calf with a hammer. The intention of Aaron was really to restrain the people until Moses came down, but Moses thought that Aaron was a partner in their crime and he was incensed against him. Whereupon God said to Moses, "I know that Aaron's intention was quite good."
>
> (Exodus Rabbah 37:2)

The possibility of Aaron's innocence is stunning. Doubters may not be moved by the Rabbis' interpretation, but the Rabbis' midrash doesn't have to satisfy everyone. It only has to open up the possibility that what Aaron was doing could not be entirely understood, except by God. Their proof is found in what is written in the Torah, when Moses was told, "You shall bring forward your brother, Aaron." The midrash teaches two points about the dilemma Moses and Aaron experienced and the solution that reconciled their relationship and their roles.

First, it's obvious from Torah that Aaron was integral to the building of the Golden Calf. Without his direction and instruction it would not have been crafted. But, even if that were the only fact in the matter, it doesn't explain why Aaron wasn't destroyed with the others who participated in the terrible sin. The fact is that Aaron survived the incident. To make the account work, something else must have been going on that Moses could not have known. The point is that Moses could only draw inferences from Aaron's deeds. What he saw was a sinful act, but it didn't explain the real reason behind his deed.

Next, the midrash teaches that while Moses could only know Aaron's deeds, God could know both Aaron's deeds and his intentions. Therefore, it makes sense that God did not kill Aaron along with his fellow Israelites, since God knew his true intentions. But we're not finished. The brilliance of the Torah text and the midrash also helps us understand why it was Moses, and not God, who called Aaron forward for service.

The principle *mipnei darchei shalom*, "for the sake of peace," is at work here. On the one hand, despite God's verdict of innocence, Aaron felt reluctant to step forward on his own to perform his duties. He was especially reluctant to step forward because his brother, Moses, had not yet exonerated him. When Moses came forward to bring his brother up to service as high priest, God reconciled them and established a firm boundary between what we can know and what we cannot know about others. The future of the Israelite people's destiny depended on both Moses and Aaron, and now it was secure.

The power of that moment of reconciliation identified God as the only One who truly knows our intentions and our deeds. It restricts us from presuming to know others' intentions by limiting our power to judge others except on the performance of their deeds. The security that this arrangement provides runs deeply through our own Jewish outlook on how we are judged, and by whom.

God Knows Best

Another text teaches us that God knows us even better than we can know ourselves. God knows our wants and needs, and God hears our pleas. And God maintains boundaries to clarify for us what is revealed to us and what is concealed from us. A salient moment of revelation is at the end of the Israelites' wilderness journey, when Moses learns that the date of his death is nearing:

> The Lord said to Moses, "Behold [*hein*], the time is drawing near for you to die."
>
> (Deuteronomy 31:14)

The midrash reveals some insight into Moses's reaction to the news that his days are coming to an end. Moses rightfully explores his feelings with God about his impending death:

> Moses said before the Holy One, blessed be God, Master of the universe, "When I praised You, I said, 'Behold [*hein*], the heavens to their uttermost reaches belong to the Lord your God, the earth and all that is on it!' Now You diminish me [You began Your reference to my death with *hein*]?" God said to Moses, "You're like a bad neighbor who sees only what goes in, and not what comes out. Remember what you said about My children the Israelites, 'Behold [*hein*], the Israelites would not listen to me....' [Exodus 6:12]. Thus you maligned My children."
>
> (*Midrash Tanchuma, Vayelech* 3)

Moses thought he did everything right. He led the people through the wilderness and he obeyed God. But he assumed too much about himself and discovered that though he played by the rules and set out to do everything he could for God, there were parts of his work that he could not evaluate himself. In the larger scheme of events, Moses accomplished much. He was regarded as the greatest prophet who ever lived. But his honor was a consolation prize when he learned that his deeds did not earn him the prize he craved, namely, entering the Promised Land. Moses was only one part of the cosmic design meant for future generations of Israelite people to reveal with God's help.

In our life, we reach points in our career and personal development when we evaluate all that we have accomplished. Some of us are satisfied with what we have done. Some of us are disappointed that all our effort hasn't earned us more status, more money, or more opportunities. We struggle to fathom how the right schools and the right choices delivered us to a certain place in our life when others who started with less now have more. Not unlike Moses, we are treading on thin ice because not only are we depriving ourselves of an honest critique, but we are also maligning others with nothing more than a jealous rant about what's "fair." But "what's fair" is part of a rule book best left behind on our childhood playground. "What's fair" is now part of a more complex set of issues, choices, and variables. As it was for Moses, some things are revealed to us and others remained concealed.

This was Moses's dilemma. Ultimately, he learned that though his days were coming to an end, all that he meant to the Israelite people and to God, too, would not be lost forever. The memory of Moses lives on, and so do the deeds he helped the Israelites accomplish and for which God is uniquely grateful. Our days may not be coming to an end, but we have reached a time in our lives when we can recognize that we cannot understand everything that happens to us, nor why or how they happen.

Now it's time for an honest evaluation. Career assessment, marital counseling, and individual psychotherapy can be helpful tools. They enable us to see what we cannot always see on our own. They don't reveal God's plan for us, but they might help us close the gap between what is and what ought to be. In our real adult world, coming to terms with what God has granted us is part of admitting that God knows us better than we know ourselves.

This is nothing like the diminishing experience of hearing our parents say, "I told you so!" Between God and us, there is both discovery and privacy, grace and dignity.

Ma'arit Ayin

Since we are limited in our ability to know each other's intentions, another guiding principle helps us perform at our best. The Rabbis call it *ma'arit ayin*, or colloquially speaking, "how things appear outwardly." It's a principle we would do well to apply at home, where we face some of our greatest personal challenges. When spouses/partners lack real time to talk about their days, let alone their intimate thoughts and needs, they begin to lack the skills to read each other's cues. Whereas a raised eyebrow used to signal a provocative desire, now it might only signal dissatisfaction and suspicion. When a late evening at the office used to demonstrate an investment in a future promotion, now it might only raise concern about how we're spending our time away from home. It's unfair to jump to conclusions and unfortunate after years of partnership. So why do we tend to do it so often?

The answer to this question cannot be found unless we return to the place where God commanded Moses to call his brother forward. The reconciliation of spouses/partners can only begin when one takes the initiative to bring the other closer in without presuming anything about their intentions. We can motivate ourselves to do this when we set aside our suspicions and focus only on the deeds of our loved ones. We must look at their behavior and give them the benefit of the doubt. When spouses/partners work long hours at the office, it isn't only because they are happier at work among colleagues and friends who share their ambitions. It's also because they are ambitious. They want the promotion that will help them realize long-term goals of financial security. An associate lawyer is eager to become partner. A young banker is eager to become an investment banker. Even a young rabbi is eager to become associate and later senior in a congregation or an organization. While these roles mean larger responsibilities, they also mean greater personal income and security for the whole family, too.

Underlying their ambitions are hopes to overcome insecurity about short-term obligations and responsibilities. New parents don't work long hours to avoid children at home; they work long hours to provide for them. The dilemma is that spending more time at work and less at home deprives couples of communicating intimately about their insecurities and worries that drive them to do what they do. Without a clear explanation, equally nervous spouses/partners at home are left to their own devices and draw their own conclusions.

When spouses/partners take the time to talk about what they want and need, they help themselves accomplish together what they cannot do alone. In the case of Moses and Aaron, it was the enormous task of completing daily responsibilities in the Tabernacle, God's dwelling place in the wilderness. Without their mutual efforts, the people would have been lost to false gods and strange lands, and the destiny of the Israelite people and their covenant with God would have been forsaken. The risks couples take are not as ominous and foreboding, but the principle remains the same. Without embracing the sacred nature of their relationship and what it means to everything that flows from it, their children will not thrive, their home will not sustain them, and any work they do outside the home will be for naught.

When it becomes especially difficult to set aside what we believe are others' intentions, there is a way to ask questions without violating the boundary we learned in Torah and midrash.

When we ask, "What are you trying to accomplish when you do that?" in a tone that suggests we are truly hoping to understand them, rather than accusing them prematurely of our own ideas, we can invite others to answer us directly and honestly. A hard-working parent whose wife thinks he's spending too much time away from home might be asked to explain what he's trying to accomplish by setting work above home. Whatever the answer might be, it will more accurately explain his behavior. Rather than talk around intentions and conjecture, which can dismantle a relationship, facts and data focus the conversation and reorient the couple toward mutual goals.

Honest Measures

We all have a desire to succeed in our multiple roles. We seek feedback and evaluations from colleagues and family members. At work, this comes in the form of real data from projects and contracts we produce. At home, it comes in the form of respectful children, joyful experiences, and real love between family members. Both at home and at work, our deeds are measured. Our intentions generally follow our deeds and vice versa. But at home, where we are not evaluated every six months or every year, we would do well to measure ourselves and others only on deeds. Where we are unsure, we need to seek answers, and when those answers are not forthcoming, we should confront others with how their actions make us feel. This is a classic way to avoid judging another's intentions in exchange for owning our own feelings. Again, the discussion becomes focused on real matters and not imaginary ones.

Outside the home, we struggle to keep up, too. At our children's schools, we strive to keep up appearances—competition between parents flourishes whenever it exists among our children.

Who is smart, who is simple, who drives what, and who said what about whom are all questions that just begin to scratch the surface of conversations shared between "friends." In our attempt to do it all and keep up, we either succumb to these pressures or find ourselves standing more alone than ever before. It's not easy to take the high road in every instance. When we try too hard to accomplish too much, someone always misses out. Either our work suffers, or our children feel neglected, or our spouses turn into roommates instead of lovers. For most of us, "having it all" is not a realistic option. Not every role can be achieved with the same level of success. Choices have to be made. Will most of the success be enjoyed at work or at home? Will there be success in personal friendships and relationships? How can a measure be established so that some success can be enjoyed more often and where it matters most?

The principle of *shalom bayit*, "peace in the home," matters here. There needs to be peace between spouses/partners, children and parents, and friends and acquaintances. This is a goal that requires enormous commitment. We have to make decisions early on about what roles we will play and how much attention they each deserve. Are the small conversations between parents in the school hallways part of our formula for peace? Will another family's issues consume our time, or can we participate meaningfully without being distracted from our own responsibilities? Making decisions about where and where not to be involved can create boundaries where limited energy produces positive results and leaves more to share.

Despite its lack of excellence, our personal effort and intention to do well cannot be discounted. In reality, competent teachers or supervisors will highlight our good intentions and best efforts even if our work did not meet their every expectation. These are important cues for us to hear. At home, a genuine attempt to help cook or clean can be appreciated for the difference it made even if it didn't get the whole job done, just as was the case for Aaron. God recognized that the outcome of the Golden Calf incident was less than ideal, but in the end, Aaron's intention served a greater good. Imagine if the Golden Calf were the only measure of duty to God. It would have meant the end of the Israelite people and their purpose for leaving Egypt. The story of our covenant with God and Torah would never have been told. The purpose of highlighting Aaron's intentions provided the balance that allowed us to understand our power to measure deeds and God's power to measure everything else.

The Torah story provides us a standard by which to measure ourselves. Now we know that we can only be judged on what can be seen. What cannot be seen or known perfectly are our intentions. At best, our intentions should match our deeds. When our intentions are not clear to others, we have a duty to provide them with clarity about our work and effort. When we're asked what we were trying to accomplish, we have to answer honestly so that our deeds can be judged alongside our true intentions. Our intentions are indeed the most difficult parts of ourselves to explain, especially when they are private. They are for God, alone, to know.

7

God Honors Me

Take a calf of the herd for a sin offering and a ram for a burnt offering without blemish.

—LEVITICUS 9:2

All that God has declared to be unclean in animals God has pronounced desirable in people.

—LEVITICUS RABBAH 7:2

As we move on into later middle age, there are at least two truths we have to embrace. First, we need to recognize that the trajectory we followed after our own days in school was the one that led us to meaningful work, a busy career, and loving relationships. It earned us opportunities to achieve many of the goals we fully expected to achieve. It was part of the American dream our parents provided us or to which we gained access through personal ambition. Second, we need to acknowledge that the same trajectory has lost some momentum since we reached midlife. Now we share in the trajectories of our children and close friends, who begin to take us with them in new directions. They might live in different cities than we do, so we make time to see them there. They still call us with their needs and worries, so we connect from a distance with as much love and concern as possible. We also share in the trajectories of our spouses/partners, where consequences of work and health bear down on us, too, for good and for ill. In the past, good health and opportunities meant that we could look far into the future and anticipate attaining everything we believed was possible. Changes at home, at work, and in our health bring about new challenges that alter our immediate and future plans.

At this particular stage in life, we are facing events we never imagined possible. If we have children, they are succeeding but also failing. In our marriages and friendships, we are finding new meaning or we are suffering. Our health is either good or slowly beginning to make us feel older than we are. The vicissitudes of life are catching up with us, not because we are at fault or because we have done something wrong, but more often simply because "life happens." We wonder if we're still acceptable to our spouse/partner, if we are sexy enough, and if we matter anymore to our children and friends. The answers we need come to us when we can first accept that we are entirely and unequivocally acceptable to God.

If we have children, they have grown up and moved away. Years ago, older adults would comment, "Cherish the time with your young children. They grow up faster than you think." In the midst of diapers, long nights with sick children, and weekends with busy schedules, we longed for time alone and quiet nights. We thought it couldn't happen fast enough. And then it happened, sooner than we thought it would, and we are left alone in our empty nest—feathered nicely, but a bit larger now that the children are gone, and quieter than it has ever been.

Now there is more time for uninterrupted conversation with our contemporaries and more time for matters of faith and Judaism. Conversations with partners and friends and introspection about religion and spirituality are, for many, positive pursuits. They can lead to deeper loves and friendships, as well as richer spiritual experiences. In this chapter, we learn that God does not need us to be perfect in order to accept us. It is only what we bring of ourselves that truly matters. Our renewed dialogue with God should reflect the depth of our wants and needs, our struggles and our strivings. As we see life for what it is and not only for what it ought to be, honesty prevails. God loves honesty. Despite our brokenness, and unlike anyone else in our life, God is strong enough to receive us and to honor us.

Accepting Imperfection

In the book of Leviticus, we read about the sacrifices our ancestors used to bring to the Temple for offerings of various kinds. Though we are far from the age of animal sacrifice, the Rabbis used these texts to extrapolate what we need to know about our relationship with God as our life and our bodies change with age.

In Leviticus, the book that outlines how to maintain a sacred community and earn God's blessing, we learn about the kinds of offerings our ancestors were commanded to bring to God:

> On the eighth day Moses called Aaron and his sons, and the elders of Israel. He said to Aaron: "Take a calf of the herd for a sin offering and a ram for a burnt offering, without blemish, and bring them before the Lord...."
> They brought to the front of the Tent of Meeting the things that Moses had commanded, and the whole community came forward and stood before the Lord. Moses said: "This is what the Lord has commanded that you do, that the Presence of the Lord may appear to you."
> (Leviticus 9:1–2, 9:5–6)

The key words in the Torah text are "without blemish." Though we have dealt with these words before, in this chapter we need to separate the offerings we bring from the one who offers them. As we learned in chapter 5, the text is clear that the offerings we bring to God, be they animals of the past or prayers of the present, should be perfect. It is in the midrash where we learn about the quality and well-being of the people who offer them:

> Rabbi Abba ben Yudan said: All that God has declared to be unclean in animals He has pronounced desirable [*kasher*] in men. In animals He has declared blind or broken or maimed or having a wen to be unserviceable, but in men He has declared the broken and crushed heart to be desirable. Rabbi Alexandri said: If a private person uses broken vessels, it is a disgrace to him, but God uses broken vessels, as it is said, "The Lord is close to the brokenhearted; those crushed in spirit [God] delivers" (Psalm 34:19); "I dwell on high, in holiness; yet with the contrite and the lowly in spirit—reviving the spirits of the lowly, reviving the hearts of the contrite" (Isaiah 57:15); "[God] heals their broken hearts and binds up their wounds" (Psalm 147:3).
>
> (Leviticus Rabbah 7:2)

Early images of God were cemented for us when we came to synagogue for worship on Shabbat and holidays. We dressed up for special occasions at the synagogue. From an early age, we believed that we could appear before God only when we were at our best, especially on the outside where clean clothes and groomed hair made a difference. From the Torah text alone, we know this is not accurate. When Moses told the people to bring offerings "without blemish," he did not add, "And comb your hair and sit up straight." When the Israelites came with their offerings, it was as if "the whole community came forward and stood before the Lord" (Leviticus 9:5). Everyone who had something to bring was welcome there.

There is no record of what condition the people who responded to Moses's words and God's command were in. We rely on the midrash to interpret the command and make clear who it is that God welcomes. Remarkably, but not surprisingly at this point, all of us are welcome no matter our condition. In fact, the broken among us are more than welcome. The verses from the Bible cited in the midrash are the proof texts the Rabbis used to make their point.

While an animal's imperfections or a prayer's inconsistencies render them unacceptable offerings to God, the same traits are considered "desirable" in people. About people, God finds desirable the "brokenhearted" and "crushed" (Psalm 34:19). The midrash uses the word *kasher* to define the difference precisely. *Kasher* doesn't only mean food that observant Jews eat. It means anything that is "fit" for use to fulfill God's commandments about food, worship, or behavior. In this context, people who are *kasher* are fit to come before God. Just as it was true in Moses's day when the community stood before God, so it is in our day when we want to come before God privately.

Holy Brokenness

In our effort to mature our image of God, we need to see our brokenness, in whatever form it is found, as a means to and not a barrier from a renewed relationship with God. Years ago, a couple I knew found their way to a deeper spiritual life as a result of their significant brokenness. They had been married for about thirty years and had truly lived the American midwestern dream. They had a successful business and a modest but lovely home, and their children were grown and on their own. Now, complications from the husband's diabetes began to pose problems for him. In and out of doctors' offices, he learned more about his disease and the creeping effects that were threatening his health. Unfortunately, he had not been disciplined about his food choices. Talks from his doctor and his wife did not impress him enough to change his habits while there was still time. Eventually, as he was told would happen, his diabetes became severely life-threatening. Well beyond other complications from diabetes, he now required surgery to save his life. Both his legs would be amputated to stop the debilitating effects of the disease.

The day of surgery came. It was a long and trying day, but the surgery was successful, and he recuperated enough to be in a regular hospital room sooner than expected. The next phase, which proved to be the biggest one of them all, was for his wife to see her husband for the first time without the full length of his legs. Until now, she had held herself back from seeing him; she was uncertain that she would find his "brokenness" desirable. She feared that she wouldn't love him anymore. She began to believe that she would lose not only the person she used to hold, but also the person she used to love.

On the day she planned to see her husband in the hospital room, she called me to help her. We met in the hallway outside his room. Standing alone, I decided to relate to her the lesson from Torah and the Rabbis' insights. "God uses broken vessels," I explained. She began to understand that while her husband was now "broken" in her eyes, God would see in him a whole human being who was still fit for service as a husband, father, and friend. Furthermore, she learned that not all brokenness is physical. There is brokenness that is unseen by us because it's internal. We're broken because we're insecure, unsure, and unfit. But these are only limitations that hold us back from each other or our given tasks. They are not impediments to our relationship with God.

The man's wife recognized that she was broken, too. She wasn't broken in physical ways like her husband, but she admitted that she wasn't perfect, either. She smiled about some of the ways she could do better. She also agreed that none of her own shortcomings were impediments to the relationship she had come to enjoy with God. Surely, she didn't want to claim that her husband couldn't have the same expectations for his relationship with God. She also didn't want to judge her husband harsher than God would judge him.

As she understood how to imagine God under these new circumstances, she became encouraged and inspired. "Are you ready to meet your husband again, for the first time?" I asked her. She nodded that she was, and we approached the door to his hospital room, together. She entered the room. It wasn't but a few minutes before they were talking openly, embracing one another, and preparing for the next chapter they would face, together.

God honored them. The wholeness they would come to know again was in large part due to their more mature image of God. At first, it seemed that God only welcomed well-dressed worshipers. Now, like our ancestors, people of all stripes whose brokenness is obvious or hidden from view are welcome before God. The prayers this couple shared were of one voice now, and they felt able to bring them to God, who hears them, too. Many weeks after his surgery and rehabilitation, the husband surprised the congregation when he opened the door to the synagogue and walked into the sanctuary on his new prosthetic legs. His friends surrounded him with careful embraces and generous amounts of admiration. He found his seat next to his wife and began to join in Shabbat services with a fuller heart and a perfect offering, despite his broken body.

Knowing You Are Loved

Physical brokenness, such as a man with amputated legs, is difficult to hide or overcome. But another, more common brokenness is found in almost all of us—the insecurities or other faults that come with age and time. At midlife, we have real reason to feel concerned about how we have spent our time and how much time we still have left. At best, insecurity can motivate us to overcome these anxieties with new initiatives and interests. Every New Year, whether Jewish or secular, many of us make resolutions to get fit, lose weight, or find love. Whatever it is, the brokenness within us can become our motivation to fix it in the future. But some brokenness can be debilitating. Midlife, the place in time that helps us see what we've accomplished, can also make us feel that we haven't achieved enough. And if we've suddenly found ourselves in ill health, in a struggling marriage, or facing family issues we didn't anticipate, then being overwhelmed by our circumstances can prevent us from finding our strength and moving on.

The wife of the ill man provides us insight into what we can do with our unseen brokenness. As she came to know for herself, no one is perfect. Everyone struggles with an issue that bombards the senses almost daily. The therapies that we seek to overcome them or to understand them can help us be more productive in our life at home and at work. They are an essential part of our healing. They are also part of the ways that we demonstrate how God honors us. We cannot deprive ourselves of the help that we need. We must strive to overcome our weaknesses and obstacles so that we can live a fuller life. There is no value in suffering unless it teaches us something about how to choose life and to live it. The Torah teaches us that God's presence is with us in our wholeness and our brokenness. It is only we who fail to recognize our worth when we are broken. We hide from others like we hide from God. We do not have to do either. Like the woman who met her husband again for the first time, we need to reveal ourselves to the ones who mean the most to us.

When we reveal ourselves to loved ones, we show them that we value their ability to care for us. We show them that we need them and that we are, in return, able to be loved and to love them back. This is what we learn in *Pirkei Avot* 3:18, where Rabbi Akiva taught, "It is one thing to be loved; it is another thing to know that you are loved." To "be loved" is about the present when a loved one embraces us. To "know that you are loved" means that the love you have shared for a lifetime goes with you wherever you are.

Most of our life is experienced through encounters with others. But there are also times when we seek to be alone with God, when only God's presence can assure us. In the course of a lifetime, many individuals seek out spiritual moments they think can only be found far from home or familiar places. Retreats, meditation rooms, and alternative worship have been the salve to heal wounds perpetrated by organized religion. In some cases, our houses of worship where we grew up or shared special moments have suffered because they couldn't meet our needs. And yet, Torah and midrash assure us that our houses of worship, like our homes and our hearts, are always capable of providing the encounters we seek. As in ancient times, it is not the person or the place, but rather the quality of the offering that we bring that is required.

After we dedicate so many years to work and serving others, it is no wonder that our personal feelings for God and religion may be weakened or rusty. Once, a young rabbi, reporting on his weekend student pulpit experience, described a worshiper who sat with his eyes closed during the sermon. The young rabbi sought input from his teacher about the incident. While it's always possible that the worshiper had no interest in the student rabbi's message, it was also possible, the teacher explained, that the worshiper had his own way of listening, considering, and pondering the message. It was also possible that the worshiper was taking the time for his own private thoughts, ill-timed as it was during the sermon.

Look around your own sanctuary during worship. How many people hold the prayer book in their hands? How many people participate or try to read or sing along? Today, worship is not only for experts. The newest prayer books include transliteration and commentaries that invite everyone into more meaningful prayer time, including the rustiest worshiper.

Our Rabbis taught us that there are two kinds of prayer: *keva* and *kavanah*. *Keva* describes the fixed prayers that are part of the regular structure or rubric of worship services. *Kavanah* describes the soulful intention of our prayers, or what is also called *tefilat halev*, "prayer of the heart." The two kinds of prayer are both important. *Keva* provides a place for all of us to share in worship. For example, the *Shema* unites us in our prayer about the One God, and the *Amidah* begins with our focus on our patriarchs and matriarchs. The order of the service, too, unites us in the way our prayers are offered to God. *Kavanah*, on the other hand, gives us room for personal expression and the ability to reach God with our separate voices. Some have debated which is more important, *keva* or *kavanah*. No one disputes the importance of *keva* to a worshiping community, but *kavanah* wins as the defining purpose for every person in his or her own quest to seek God.

From my own vantage point on the pulpit, I observe many kinds of worshipers. One woman in particular is a regular worshiper on the Sabbath, yet she never opens the prayer book. She once explained that because she knew the prayers by heart, she had no need to open the book. This became a teachable moment when I recalled what our Rabbis also taught us about daily prayer. Familiar prayers are *keva*, fixed in tradition, but it is up to us to bring something new of ourselves to those prayers every day. It is our *kavanah* that makes the words on the page sing a new song to God, as it were, and rise with all our soulfulness as a perfect offering of our hearts. The worshiper nodded approvingly and in appreciation.

It is gratifying to know that Judaism celebrates personal prayer and not only on the tops of beautiful mountains or in the midst of inspiring weekend retreats. While they have their purpose, retreats are not substitutes for what is still available to us in the sanctuary, at home, and always in our hearts. God honors God's creations, with all of our imperfections and inconsistencies. As the midrash makes clear in verses cited from the Bible, God honors "the contrite and the lowly in spirit," and "heals their broken hearts and binds up their wounds." Furthermore, although midrash has already taught us that God is everywhere, the Bible explains that God does this from "on high," where God "dwells in holiness." The contrast demonstrated in the text makes the lesson that much more meaningful. As One who dwells on high, away from earthly matters, God's reach finds us and brings us up to stand in God's presence.

Brokenness in our life is not only a matter of infirmity. There are many struggles we face when we reach midlife. It is at that juncture when we look back and forward at the same time. There is much we can see in hindsight, and this leaves us either satisfied or disappointed, or both. The Torah and midrash help us see that we can be at peace with the place we have reached. We are attractive to our spouse/partner. We're even sexy. We're also vital to our adult children, who need us even if they struggle to say so when we need to hear it most. We need not be perfect or whole in body or spirit to seek meaning in life. We do so in God's presence, where God honors us every day.

8

God Receives Me

Turn back, O rebellious children, I will heal your afflictions!

—JEREMIAH 3:22

Return to me, repent, and I will receive you.

—*PESIKTA RABBATI* 44:9

Years have passed in which we have focused on everyone else's needs. Whoever depended on us—coworkers or family members—might still need us, but not the way they used to in the past. We gave them everything they needed, and now they're doing exactly what we wished they would do. The house is quieter. We hear from our children, who call to share their lives and visit on the holidays. We have more time on our hands than ever before, and yet it's still not enough to fill the new void that resides deep inside us. Where did this empty feeling come from? How did we go from being busy and needed to available and optional?

Whatever our personal circumstances, this period of later middle age has the distinct possibility of being a time to reclaim the relationship with God that is still available to us. As with most life-altering journeys, taking new steps can be the most challenging. Turning to God in newer or deeper ways might feel foreign. While we were attending to many needs at home and at work, we either succeeded or failed to maintain some level of religious observance. However we might measure it, our deepest sense of faith probably came through our relationships with others and our duty to them. Children were blessed by the rabbi, given a Jewish education in day school or religious school, and called to Torah as a bar or bat mitzvah. Perhaps we also accompanied them to the *chuppah* (marriage canopy) and set them on a path of good deeds. But doing the *mitzvah* for the sake of the *mitzvah*, while a reward in and of itself, without also taking notice of God in our own life, deprived us of maturing our image of God as we matured over the years.

Like childhood games that occupied us on a rainy day but didn't hold our interest as we grew up, God was shelved after our obligations to listen to our parents and Jewish teachers ended. Our vague notions of God may have sustained us when we provided for others. But now that we are alone with ourselves and dormant God images are taking on new life, what is left of that image of God? Instead of nurturing it over the years, we found other ways to exercise our spiritual interests. Popular trends in exercise, spa treatments, and alternative meditation gave us some serenity, nourishment, and peace. Sometimes they worked. More often, they cost a fortune and led to yet more treatments and purchases. These experiences weren't meaningless, but they passed as soon as the spa closed and its proprietors moved on. By contrast, God is free and never closes. We can return and reclaim our relationship with God while we mature it for our life today.

Repairing Relationships

Honest individuals may admit that they were not necessarily faithful to God in Judaism as they aged. Coming back to God after years of estrangement might make us feel as if we were an unfaithful spouse returning home to reclaim something we spurned. Just as there are spousal relationships that fail due to infidelity and some that can be retrieved and saved with acts of *teshuvah*, "repentance," so the covenantal relationship God made with our ancestors and with us can also be repaired when it breaks and fails. The difference is that while a lover may not forgive a partner who has strayed, we are always welcome back to our spiritual place and home with God.

An important example is found in the book of Jeremiah. There the prophet speaks to the Israelite people about their infidelity to God and what can become of them:

> [The word of the Lord came to me] as follows: If a man divorces his wife, and she leaves him and marries another man, can he ever go back to her? Would not such a land be defiled? Now you have whored with many lovers: can you return to Me?—says the Lord.... Turn back, O rebellious children, I will heal your afflictions!
>
> (Jeremiah 3:1, 3:22)

The prophet makes it clear that though Israel has "whored with many lovers [gods]," they can still turn back. God will heal their afflictions. This has always been the hope throughout the ages since the covenant was sealed at Mount Sinai. Though the people were unfaithful and they knew other gods, their way back to God was never closed to them. Our hope is retrieved by the Rabbis, who taught us that the enduring covenant is still available to us even after all these years and despite our wanderings. The midrash makes the point perfectly clear:

> But God is not so. Even though Israel has deserted Lord, and served other gods, God says: Return to Me, repent, and I will receive you. So Jeremiah, too, applies the same contrast, and says: Though you have played the harlot with many lovers, yet return again to me and I will receive you.
>
> (*Pesikta Rabbati* 184a)

The biblical verses are more akin to our own experiences where infidelity occurs. Long before there is any hope of reconciliation between unfaithful partners, revelations about affairs expose us to untold scrutiny and scorn. Couples who have experienced such pain can recover, but they can't forget the humiliation and sore feelings. Sometimes the only way to distance themselves from the embarrassment and emotional pain is to split permanently and go physically to new locales. Oddly enough, the opposite is true in our relationship with God. Rather than split permanently and retreat to new locations, God says, "Return to Me, and I will receive you." In the wake of estrangement, God encourages us to come even closer than before, affirming the depth of God's love and hope for us.

Taking Action

Those who return to God often begin with a return to the synagogue. It isn't unusual for a potential member of a synagogue to come see the rabbi. When I meet potential members of the synagogue, I begin with the obvious question, "What interests you?" Answers can vary, naturally, but the one that expresses deep-seated needs to reconnect with God and Judaism always sounds like this: "I'm not sure I am eligible to be a member." It's not really an answer to the question, but it says much about the visitor. He or she is really asking, "Do I qualify?" It's a guarded question that's often followed by, "I'm not sure I believe in God." For him or her, this question is a litmus test for membership. In return, I ask, "Do you believe in the possibility of God?" Every time, the answer is, "Yes, I believe in the possibility of God." Still, the answer is not a solution. The answer is only a starting point that brings us together at a point on a journey. Now the role of a rabbi is to be a teacher, a mentor, and a guide.

In Judaism, God is not found. God is sought. So, let's not grow concerned about "finding" God while we search for God again. Seeking can begin in the synagogue, because it's a resource for worship, study, and community. But the synagogue is not as central in Judaism as the home itself. Exactly where we need to feel less alone is precisely the place Judaism elevates to the highest level. Our Rabbis taught that the home is considered to be a *mikdash me'at*, "a small sanctuary," like the *Mikdash*, or Tabernacle, that God commanded the Israelites to build in the wilderness. God's intention is to dwell with us in our own "small sanctuaries," accompanying us "when we lie down, when we rise up," and along the way. The home, where we raise our children and where we feed our own spiritual hunger, is not the *Mikdash*, the Tabernacle, but a *mikdash me'at*, a small sanctuary that serves a similar purpose. It serves us on our own journey. It's a great comfort to know that God is available to us not only in the synagogue. It's a great relief to know that when we come home at the end of the day to a quiet house, we're not really alone at all, because God is there.

Still, it isn't enough just to call our home a small sanctuary where God can be found. As a people of faith, we are more often a people of action first. Our propensity for action is exemplified by the way the Israelites stood at Mount Sinai and pledged their commitment to God, when they said in one voice, *Na'aseh v'nishma*. "We will faithfully do" (Exodus 24:7). The translation doesn't do justice to the meaning of the Hebrew. *Na'aseh* means "we will do." *Nishma* means "we will obey and understand." The order of the words is significant. Notice that the Israelites pledged to *do* everything that God commanded first, and to obey and *understand* it later. There is no profession, trade, or license that would be granted in modern times to do anything without first demonstrating proficiency and skill. Would you go to a doctor who pledged to "do" first and "understand" later? Would you vote for a politician without any idea of his or her record of service? Would you be granted a diploma just for showing up? For that matter, would you buy a car only on word of mouth without also taking a test drive? Of course not. The Israelites' declaration was an extraordinary act of unequivocal faith. But it also set an example of how Judaism is lived.

As a religion of action, Jews are prompted by the prophets' calls to feed the hungry, clothe the naked, and house the homeless. Our Rabbis call on us to repair the world (*tikkun olam*). We have inherited a long history of doing first and understanding later. The Rabbis taught us that our understanding comes through doing. To our point, the adult God seeker should not have to study everything there is to know or learn everything there is to do before beginning to take action. A teacher, a guide, or a mentor can easily facilitate Jewish participation. Jewish understanding will be up to individuals according to their ability.

Judaism is surely known for its intellectual pursuits. Those who are so inclined will be nourished by centuries of Jewish wisdom. But God seekers are not only intellectuals. They can also be purely doers. Because understanding and spirituality come through the doing, very active Jewish volunteers, worshipers, teachers, students, and so on find their lives full and satisfying through the roles they choose to play in their local Jewish communities. Still, one of the best places to claim God for ourselves is at home.

A classic answer to the classic question, "Where do I find God?" is "Wherever you let God in." At home, letting God in begins with doing. One of the first acts performed by Jewish homeowners is affixing the mezuzah, the unique holder of the Torah texts that teach us, "Inscribe them [Torah] on the doorposts of your house" (Deuteronomy 6:9). The simple act of affixing the mezuzah fulfills the expectation from Psalms, "Unless the Lord builds the house, its builders toil in vain" (Psalm 127:1). Once a mezuzah is in place, every time the family or visitors enter or exit the house, there is a constant reminder of God's presence and of our personal duty to mind our deeds and our words, helping us reach our goal of keeping a sacred home and building a sacred life.

Another way to bring God into our home is by celebrating Shabbat and taking a weekly break from work. By focusing on ourselves as God's creations, we sanctify our lives and bring ourselves closer to God. Shabbat blessings are not difficult to do. They are easily found in most prayer books in both Hebrew and English, along with simple directions about how to kindle the lights and recite the *Kiddush* (blessing over the wine) and *HaMotzi* (blessing over the bread). Rabbi David Polish explains that when we light the Sabbath candles, "what was only episodic becomes epochal, and what was only a moment in Jewish history becomes eternal in Jewish life."[3] His point is that the single moment of participating in the ancient ritual of lighting the Sabbath candles connects us with Jews everywhere in the world today and with those who came before us in the past. He explains that the ritual of making the Sabbath connects us to Abraham and Sarah, Isaac and Rebecca, and to Jacob, Leah, and Rachel, whose God is also our God.

Meeting God Halfway

The promise is clear that God receives us, but what if we're not up to the task of seeking God? What if we can intellectualize the message but fail to realize the goal? If it all depended on us, then the prophet's promise that God receives us would still be a conditional one. The Rabbis understood this dilemma and resolved it with a parable:

> A prince was far away from his father—a hundred days' journey away. His friends said to him, "Return to your father." He replied, "I cannot; I don't have the strength." Thereupon his father sent word, saying to him, "Come back as far as you can according to your strength, and I will go the rest of the way to meet you." So the Holy One, blessed be God, says to Israel, "Return to Me, and I will return to you" (Malachi 3:7).
>
> (*Pesikta Rabbati* 44:9)

It is one thing to say, "Come home"; it's another thing to say, "I'll meet you halfway." So, the Rabbis taught that God's promise to receive us came with an incentive. Instead of God waiting for us to come all the way back, God will meet us wherever we are. That's the reason why a litmus test for membership in a synagogue is useless. That's why the journey begins exactly where we are on our path in life. That's also why the rabbi, the Jewish master teacher, meets us where we are.

God comes to us where we are so that we are not required to make the whole journey on our own. That's a real promise to be received by God. Like an unconditionally loving parent, God receives us. Unlike a parent who uses tough love appropriately to define boundaries for an errant child, God is able to receive us even when we are seeking God and can't yet come all the way on our own. And if that were not enough, God is still willing to receive us after we have gone "whoring around," seeking other gods, as the prophet put it.

Our image of God takes on many personal dimensions now. God doesn't replace our children who have moved away from home. Rather, God reappears in ways that we never saw God in the past, not because God wasn't there, but because *we* weren't there. We weren't available. Again, it wasn't a sin. Let's give ourselves credit for what we've accomplished. Let's boost ourselves up and recognize what we have done in our own way on our own terms. Within wide and reasonable boundaries, we did well.

We all have memories of our children when they were young. We play back the tapes of cherished times and events. We wouldn't deprive them of their new status as adults, but we can't help struggling to reclaim a part of their youth, and ours. When we drive down the street and see young parents walking with their children skipping just a few steps ahead of them, we want to stop and stare. It's surreal how much we've aged. Those parents and their children represent all of us who experienced the blur of time that turns small children into grown adults.

Looking back, we also remember the Jewish events we experienced with our families. We recall that God's presence was an important part of the moment. There isn't a more poignant example of being in God's presence than the day of our children's bar or bat mitzvah. This is the moment when all the hard work of thirteen years is presented for all to see. From the bimah, parents don't say, "It's a wonder he ever made it," even if it is. Rather, parents often report that their son or daughter is the most remarkable, empathetic, and brilliant child in the world.

In my synagogue, on Friday evenings just before we take our places on the bimah, we share a blessing with the bar or bat mitzvah child, the parents and grandparents, and in many cases great-grandparents, too. We take a moment to acknowledge the personal effort that went into reaching this milestone experience. At that moment, family members are often overwhelmed with feelings of gratitude. Whether or not they are perfect believers in God, they see in front of them the blessings of their children. So as not to brush off the significance of the moment, we recite the *Shehecheyanu* prayer, which thanks God "for keeping us in life, for sustaining us, and for enabling us to reaching this time."

Similar emotions take hold at weddings. The overwhelming sense of joy and gladness that parents and grandparents express at family weddings is undeniably spiritual. These overwhelming feelings come from a place deep within us in which we feel connected to a rhythm of humanity in the universe. We need not understand it completely nor lay claim to its creation. The joy and sorrow of transitions leave us both grateful and reminiscent as we step forward into the next stage of our life's journey.

Just when we find ourselves searching for our place in a wide world, God receives us openly and without reservations, meeting us wherever we may be. Unlike any reconciliation with a spouse/partner, a relative, or a friend, this reconciliation exposes us without pain and embarrassment. As we move into our later years, our image of God comes into greater focus for us. Unencumbered by many others' needs, we can now consider our own perspective on our life. Looking back is not always easy, especially when there are regrets or missed opportunities, but now we can see them as choices we made along the way. We are the product of our life experiences. How we choose to learn from them is still up to us. Our image of God can benefit from perspective and hindsight, as well as foresight. We're free to ask new questions, such as: What do we need at this stage in our life? Where will we take God with us today? The journey continues as we seek God and God receives us.

9

God Comforts Me

"You shall circumcise the flesh of your foreskin, and that shall be the sign of the covenant between Me and you."
—GENESIS 17:11

The Lord appeared to [Abraham] by the terebinths of Mamre; he was sitting at the entrance of the tent as the day grew hot.
—GENESIS 18:1

"Before this, uncircumcised mortals visited you; but now I and My retinue will appear to you."
—GENESIS RABBAH 48:9

Moses lived to be 120 years old. To this day, to wish someone a long life, it's customary to tell them, "May you live *ad me'ah v'esrim*, to be 120 years old." It used to be that living to 100 was so far from reality that to wish someone 120 years was a very generous concept. Today, as we live longer than ever before, it isn't unusual for those of us who enjoy relatively good health and good genes to live well into our 90s. But to anyone who is in their 90s, it isn't uncommon for them to respond to the customary wish to live to be 120, "Only in good health." They have already come to experience the effects of living longer. They can account for many positive experiences they have had with family, extended family, and countless friends. They have traveled far and near, read and studied, tasted and sensed marvelous foods, sights, and sounds. They have made a difference, and they are able to derive much satisfaction from many parts of their life. Now, the body is not what it used to be. The mind is sharp but the body struggles, or the body is strong and the mind struggles. We discover new limits based on our strength and our will. Ironically, though our faculties fade over time, our faith is more resilient than ever. It comes at a time in our life when we need it most.

Abraham's Old Age

In Torah, we learn that Abraham, ever the man of faith, came to learn more about his covenant with God in his later years than in his youth. We met Abraham when he smashed his father's idols and later embarked on his journey of faith. Then, at the age of ninety-nine, God appeared to him and said, "I will establish My covenant between Me and you, and I will make you exceedingly numerous" (Genesis 17:2). This is the point in the Torah narrative when God changes Abram's name to Abraham, and God makes him the father of "a multitude of nations." Furthermore, God seals the covenant with a physical sign, the circumcision:

> "As for you, you and your offspring to come throughout the ages shall keep My covenant. Such shall be the covenant between Me and you and your offspring to follow which you shall keep: every male among you shall be circumcised. You shall circumcise the flesh of your foreskin, and that shall be the sign of the covenant

between Me and you. And throughout the generations, every male among you shall be circumcised at the age of eight days."

(Genesis 17:9–12)

Abraham circumcised himself at the age of ninety-nine. Ever since, every Jewish boy is circumcised on the eighth day of his life, health permitting. Abraham's age when he circumcised himself is significant to us. Biblical ages are not calculated or understood like ours today, but there is little doubt that Abraham was advanced in years, and he bore the full brunt of the commandment. We read about the day after Abraham's circumcision:

The Lord appeared to him by the terebinths of Mamre; he was sitting at the entrance of the tent in the heat of the day. Looking up, he saw three men standing near him. As soon as he saw them, he ran from the entrance of the tent to greet them and, bowing to the ground, he said, "My lords, if it please you, do not go on past your servant. Let a little water be brought; bathe your feet and recline under the tree. And let me fetch a morsel of bread that you may refresh yourselves; then go on, seeing that you have come your servant's way." They replied, "Do as you have said."

(Genesis 18:1–5)

Here, just after Abraham performed the ritual act of circumcision on himself, God appeared to Abraham. Visits from God to Abraham were not unusual. But today, he was sitting at the entrance of the tent as the day grew hot. It was reaching mid-afternoon, when a Middle Eastern sun was especially hot. Then Abraham looked up and saw three men standing near him. The

Torah has just claimed that none other than God appeared to him, and so the commentators explain that these three visitors were actually angels, emissaries of God. This was something entirely new for Abraham and for the faith he and his descendants would know. Here, God's visit came after the first circumcision, the oldest ongoing religious ritual of all time.

Abraham's faith was tested here. Not only did he circumcise himself as a sign of the covenant, along with all the males in his camp, but Abraham also longed to welcome guests, an integral aspect of his religious lifestyle. Up until this time, visitors used to make frequent visits to his tent. Now, after his selfless act of circumcision, no one came to see him:

> Abraham complained, "Before I was circumcised travelers used to visit me; now that I am circumcised they will no longer visit me?" Said God to Abraham, "Before this, uncircumcised mortals visited you; but now I and My retinue will appear to you." Thus, "And he lifted up his eyes and looked [Genesis 18:2]," he saw the *Shechinah* [divine presence] and saw the angels.
>
> (Genesis Rabbah 48:9)

The appearance of the angels restores Abraham's faith, much as we hope ours will be in our later years. At the age of ninety-nine, Abraham had already fulfilled a lifetime of deeds. But when he fulfilled the act of circumcision, one of the greatest commandments, he felt ignored and forgotten. When God and God's angels visited Abraham at his tent in the heat of the day, he was still healing from his circumcision. He was alone. No doubt, he felt disconnected from others and especially from his faith in God, who had led him, thus far, to this place and time. Their visit restored Abraham's faith that *mitzvot*, "commandments," and a life dedicated to *mitzvot* did not distance him from God; rather, they brought him closer to God, and God closer to him. There was no better demonstration of God's compassion than a personal home visit when Abraham was healing.

Visiting the Sick

The lesson for Abraham is not lost on us. It is important to anticipate that God's comfort is available to us in our senior years. These are the times in our life when we want to know that God is present for us no matter our level of religious observance in our lifetime. Those of us who were observant might feel a kinship with God that brings us immediate comfort when we are ailing and healing. Those of us who were not observant or truly wandering in faith might feel uncertain that God's comfort is available also to us. But we have already learned that God meets us where we are on our life's journey. God receives us even after we have gone astray in our search for religious meaning.

At any time in our life, but especially when we are seniors, illness and infirmity can mean time in the hospital. It can also mean one of the most desperate times in our life. We are older. We heal less quickly. We have not necessarily "made peace" with God, and we wonder now, more than ever, how to gain access to that relationship in order to find healing of body, mind, and soul.

One of the many seniors I have visited in the hospital—I'll call him Max—expressed many of these common concerns. When I entered the room and identified myself to him, he welcomed me. He spoke up almost immediately and made three comments before I could even begin our conversation. He said, "Thank you for coming to see me," "I'm sorry I haven't been to worship services more often," and finally, "Why has God abandoned me?" His first two comments required only a truthful and thoughtful response. I told him that it's a duty to visit the sick. In his case, it was also a pleasure to see him. I also explained that attendance at worship services is not recorded, nor does it change the purpose of my visit. The question about God's presence, however, was a comment that required a patient answer. Without one, he would have suffered spiritually, worrying that he had done something to offend God, causing his illness, or that his lack of faith might prevent his recovery. What's more, any rabbi's visit can suggest to some patients that their condition is worse than it is or worse than they were originally told. Some patients refuse a rabbi's visit for that reason.

I stood at Max's bedside and spoke softly and patiently with him. Briefly, I recounted to him the story of Abraham, who circumcised himself at the age of ninety-nine. Not only did visitors come when Abraham was infirm, but also his first visitors were God's angels. Like Abraham, anyone who spends his or her life doing good deeds can expect to be rewarded with the knowledge that God comforts us in the time of our healing. Max smiled at the notion that God could be a source of comfort to him. Now he struggled with the image of God he had held for so long. It was an image that led him to believe that God was only part of joyful life events. He knew that people prayed in hospitals, but he thought it was for repentance, in order to heal so that they could find God again in happier places.

With me, Max easily recounted happy times from his past. He related how blessed he felt on birthdays, bar and bat mitzvah celebrations, weddings, and anniversaries. He spoke about his family and the number of children, grandchildren, and great-grandchildren he had. He had pictures hanging on the wall of his hospital room. He insisted on pointing them out to me. Thinking about those occasions, he readily admitted that God was in those times and places, because they were so joyful. So why was God not here, in the hospital? It was still a question he had difficulty answering for himself. Then I asked him, why do you think that God appeared to Moses in a lowly thorn bush? Wouldn't it have been a better story if God had appeared in something more joyful and beautiful, like a sycamore tree?

He didn't have an answer. He insisted that I tell him. I explained that in a midrash, the Rabbis taught us that God was in the thorn bush because if God could appear there, then God could appear anywhere. Likewise, God was in the hospital and in the midst of infirmity. God wasn't there because God causes suffering. Infirmity and disease are part of the human condition. Now, God was there as a source of everything Max needed most—courage, strength, and hope. Max began to nod his head in agreement. He began to relax. He said that it was foolish to think that God punished him. For what? Because he missed services, even though he prayed in his heart? Because he made some mistakes in his life, even though he prospered and contributed generously when he could?

Before I left him to rest in his hospital bed, I offered Max some words to recite as he prepared to sleep for the night. It was from Psalm 118:6, and the final verse from the familiar hymn *Adon Olam* (Ruler of the Universe), sung at the end of Sabbath worship in the synagogue: *Adonai li, v'lo ira*, "God is with me, I will not fear." He and many patients find that these familiar words provide a critical link between them and God.

Max appreciated the possibility that God was with him in the hospital. He was moved by the idea. He shed some tears when we prayed, "Praised are You, God, who heals the sick. May Max feel Your presence. May You help him find the courage and strength to make each day better; and may You guide the hands of those who help in healing, the doctors, nurses, and caregivers, so that Max may soon return to the company of his family and friends at home. May You bless Max with peace." His tears told me everything I needed to know. He was scared, but he was comforted. He was scared because his condition was life-threatening and he knew it. He was comforted because he had reestablished a relationship with God that met his needs. Now, Max could turn to God for everything he needed, at any time, and he believed that God would turn to him.

Abraham's extraordinary visit from God while he healed also demonstrated the duty to visit the sick. A visit relieves patients of their suffering. They feel more connected to others who share stories about familiar places, events, and friends, and by welcoming guests they are given the opportunity to perform the *mitzvah* of hospitality. For their visitors, Abraham and Sarah became gracious hosts who provided food and comfort even during their own illnesses. In effect, the visit took Abraham's mind off his own discomfort and healing process:

> Abraham hastened into the tent to Sarah, and said, "Quick, three *seahs* of choice flour! Knead and make cakes!" Then Abraham ran to the herd, took a calf, tender and choice, and gave it to a servant-boy, who hastened to prepare it. He took curds and milk and the calf that had been prepared and set these before them; and he waited on them under the tree as they ate."
>
> (Genesis 18:6–8)

God's comfort, in the form of visitors, enabled Abraham to feel at ease in his healing. It also engaged Abraham once more in a life of *mitzvah*. Even for us, the comfort we derive from believing God's presence is with us in times of infirmity can help us feel connected to others. When we feel hopeful and needed, we get active again in family activities and eventually in the community. When we feel that we're on the mend, we adopt a positive outlook. The busier we are, the faster we heal, since engaging in a familiar routine makes us feel that our presence makes a difference.

Shadow Grief

We pause in times of infirmity to reflect on our mortality. It's not easy to do, but it's human and it's normal. We remember the events that gave us joy and happiness. We remember the difficult experiences that also made us stronger some of the time. As our image of God matures with us, we understand that it is God's comfort that helps us draw meaning from the memory of those whose lives have ended, too. When we mark time on our life's journey, we want to recall those who have gone from life. Their memories are still part of us. When we recite *Yizkor*, the memorial prayers, we are asking God to remember our loved ones. God's comfort extends not only to us, but also to those whom we remember.

Such comfort can ease us through the lingering stages of mourning. Sometimes, our mourning can resurface when we become reflective about our life. When it does reappear and our sadness emerges again, one expert, Bruce Horacek, calls it "shadow grief." He describes it as

> a dull ache in the background of one's feelings that remains fairly constant and that, under certain circumstances and on certain occasions, comes bubbling to the surface, sometimes in the form of tears, sometimes not, but always accompanied by a feeling of sadness and mild sense of anxiety.[4]

What do we do to mitigate our shadow grief? A part of the answer lies in each of us. It is found in the pure soul God created in us, which remains tied to its Creator. Another source of comfort is the memory of the very people with whom we shared life-changing experiences. These memories become powerful reminders of what will always be important to us. The people we miss were those we counted on, learned from, and continue to love deeply. Yet another answer about how to mitigate shadow grief is found in a Rabbinic tale:

> The son of a rabbi mourned the death of his beloved father. Day after day, the son went to the cemetery and threw himself on the grave of his father. One day as the son gave way to fits of sorrow, his father appeared to him in a vision. His father said to him, "My son, do you think that you honor my memory with your grief? Offer me no tributes of tears. Build for me no monuments of sorrow. Do not weep for me. Live for me! Show your love by obedience to God's commandments, by devotion to faith, and by service to your fellow human beings. This," said his father, "is the memorial that truly honors the departed." After hearing these words, the son lifted himself from his father's grave, and went forth to make of his father's memory a perpetual light to guide him on paths of righteousness and truth.[5]

The rabbi gave his son a gift when he told him to keep living by honoring his father's memory through his deeds. We can assume that the son left the cemetery to pursue life and to bring honor to his father by doing so. We, too, must fulfill the meaning of our life, enriched by the memories of those who have died. Our shadow grief may linger for years, but we cannot allow it to become a stumbling block to our life. Those who remember their loved ones do so with pictures they see in their home, with a memorial plaque in temple, and with regular contributions of time or resources that help others know how his or her memory still inspires us to do and be our best. All is not lost if we regard memory as the sacred gift that it is.

God's comfort can also help take away the sting of our loss. Our loved ones provided us so much, but we were not completely dependent on them. Our life was full because of their contributions of emotional and other forms of support, but it was also full because of what we contributed to those relationships, friendships, and special bonds.

In an anonymous poem, the writer suggests that while we grow and live as children of our parents and in other loving relationships, we sometimes fail to see what they tried to give us, so that now, in their absence, we can forget what we gained and which endures beyond their lifetime. The poem, composed in both English and Yiddish, is called "All I Got Was Words":

> When I was young and fancy free,
> My folks had no fine clothes for me
> All I got was words:
>> *Got tzu danken (Thank God)*
>> *Got vet geben (God will provide)*
>> *Zol mir leben un zein gezunt (Live and be well)*
> When I was wont to travel far,
> They didn't provide me with a car
> All I got was words:
>> *Geh gezunt (Be healthy)*
>> *Geh pamelech (Go slowly)*
>> *Hub a glickliche reise (Have a good life)*

> I wanted to increase my knowledge
> But they couldn't send me to college
> All I got was words:
>> *Hub saychel (Have common sense)*
>> *Zei nischt kein narr (You are not a fool)*
>> *Torah iz di beste schorah (Torah is the best lesson)*
> The years have flown—the world has turned,
> Things I've gotten; things I've learned.
> Yet I remember:
>> *Zog dem emes (Tell the truth)*
>> *Gib Tzedakah (Give charity)*
>> *Hub Rachmonas (Have compassion)*
>> *Zei a mench! (Be a mensch, a good person)*
> All I got was words.[6]

The Yiddish words, which are not translated in the original poem, were aphorisms that were meant to be part of a rich inheritance of ideas. The poet's parents didn't have "things" to leave him; they had ideas and dreams. The poet laments that all he got was words. But we know that what he got was far more important. He knew that his parents wanted the best for him in whatever he chose for himself in his lifetime. All they really wanted for him was expressed in the words *Zei a mensch*! "Be a *mensch*!" (an exceptionally fine human being).

Surely, our own inheritance cannot be reduced to material objects or money. It is also the lessons, the words, and the experiences of our lives. Perhaps not all of them are clear and understandable, but looking back, we can raise our estimation of our loved ones when we try to see clearly now what we could not necessarily see then. Now, looking back, we see their reasons, their methods, and even their madness. When they didn't seem to give love easily, they meant well anyway; when they didn't give us the things we wanted, they gave us what they thought we needed instead. When we acknowledge their absence, we know that they are more than a memory; they are part of who we are today and who we are still on the way to becoming.

They are all, in effect, the visitors who continue to come by during times of introspection and healing. Like Abraham, we become introspective when we find ourselves sitting alone after fulfilling all the expectations not only of a loving and comforting God, but also of all the people who came to depend on us at home, work, and synagogue. Where are they now, we wonder? Is loneliness the price we pay for contributions of time and money? These are precisely the times when we seek God's comfort to remind us that we are not alone at all. Others who are busy the way we used to be are not always able to come by for a visit or to remember the ways we used to spend time together. They should call more often and visit occasionally, but it is God's presence, like the angels who visited Abraham, that can still inspire us.

A Legacy of Comfort

Our lifetime of commitment to religious duties fulfilled our covenant with God, and it was not for naught. It saw us through a lifetime of experiences that do not leave us sitting alone near the end of the journey, on a hot day, but rather secure in the faith that though our days are no longer as full as they once were, neither are we alone. It is confidence that God's comfort is with us that inspires us to get up in the morning and participate where we can with family and friends. Like Abraham and Sarah, we might get up enthusiastically to provide a meal and a place to sit for those who visit. And then, when the visit is over, we can reflect on the gift that God provided in the form of loving family and friends who came to keep us occupied and to give us a *mitzvah* to do.

As for Max, the patient we met earlier in the chapter, eventually he returned home to recuperate. He enjoyed some months before his condition ultimately worsened and he died. His family remembered a remarkable man and found comfort in the words that we recited at the funeral—*Adonai li, v'lo ira,* "God is with me, I shall not fear." They were the words he came to know for himself that described the good life he lived. They were also the words that reunited him with faith that he would never be alone. Max learned late in life that God's presence was with him everywhere and that God was, like God was for Abraham and Sarah, a source of comfort for him. Now his family is comforted as well.

10

God Strengthens Me

In Your love You lead the people You redeemed;
In Your strength You guide them to Your holy abode.
—EXODUS 15:13

"Your strength" is but a designation for the Torah.
—MECHILTA D'RABBI ISHMAEL, TRACTATE SHIRATA 5:2

We reach a point in our life when by all accounts we have the duty and the privilege to look back at the life we led. With God's help, we admit that we have come a long way. We have achieved much and made a difference where we could. Whether or not we are rich or poor, and whether or not we are pleased with our lot in life or are filled with regrets, there is a question that all of us ask ourselves: "What is the source of my strength?" Sometimes we offer clever answers, or we suggest that it's God's will. Privately, we may like to believe that the core strength that animated us and kept us grounded truly came from a sacred place.

Finding Strength in God

The answer to one of life's most profound questions is only alluded to in life-cycle events. We see strength in our children and grandchildren

and in what we were able to build over time. But the very source of
these answers cannot be found in our reminiscences alone. The source
is found in *Shirat HaYam*, the Song of the Sea, where the Israelites
rejoiced in their victory after Pharaoh and his men were drowned in
the sea. Verses from this song are a familiar part of our regular liturgy
during weekday and Sabbath worship:

> Who is like You, O Lord, among the celestials;
> Who is like You, majestic in holiness,
> Awesome in splendor, working wonders!
>
> (Exodus 15:11)

In these verses, we ask a rhetorical question that elevates and sep-
arates God from all other beings. Obviously, no one is like "You, O
Lord," even among all the gods that are worshiped by other peoples.
The source of God's own extraordinary strength is found in the
verses that follow:

> You put out Your right hand,
> The earth swallowed them.
> In Your love You lead the people You redeemed;
> In Your strength You guide them to Your holy abode.
>
> (Exodus 15:12–13)

In verse 13, the words "in Your strength" reveal that God's
power to redeem a whole nation wasn't just a miracle beyond
our comprehension. Nor was it meant to be hidden. The text
gives it away when it tells us that God achieved these great
events by means of a source of strength. What, then, is God's
strength? And if we can know what the source of that strength
is, can we have some of it, too? The midrash provides the
answer:

For the sake of the Torah that they were destined to receive, for "Your strength" here is but a designation for the Torah, as in the passage, "The Lord will give strength unto [God's] people" (Psalm 29:11).

(*Mechilta d'Rabbi Ishmael*, Tractate *Shirata* 5:2)

God's strength is Torah. Not only is it within our grasp and our comprehension, but it is also part of us and in us:

Surely, this Teaching which I enjoin upon you this day is not too baffling for you, nor is it beyond reach. It is not in the heavens, that you should say, "Who among us can go up to the heavens and get it for us and impart it to us, that we may observe it?" Neither is it beyond the sea, that you should say, "Who among us can cross to the other side of the sea and get it for us and impart it to us, that we may observe it?" No, the thing is very close to you, in your mouth and in your heart, to observe it.

(Deuteronomy 30:11–14)

Moses speaks these words to the Israelites before his death, restating what God wanted them to know about their exodus from Egypt: that God's strength redeemed and sustained them on their journey, and that the gift of Torah was "their life and the length of their days" (Deuteronomy 30:20; translation mine). The sole reason for bringing the Israelites out of Egypt was to bring them to Sinai for the sake of giving them (and all future generations through them) the Torah.

The reference to Psalm 29:11, "The Lord will give strength unto God's people," turns what could have been only a matter of faith in God's blessing for us into a tangible gift found in Torah teachings. The Rabbis believed that these words were from Sinai, dictated to Moses. Modern Jews also accept the possibility that Torah was inspired by God, but written by man. Whatever their origin, Torah teachings are the stories from which we derive all our strength as a people, along with our morals, ethics, rituals, and mission.

At this time of our life, when we can see more years behind us than ahead of us, we reflect on the lessons that guided us most and that served us best. Numerous Torah lessons and insights fill volumes of works that are often beyond our reach. More likely, we have identified certain teachings and insights that served as our moral guide and compass throughout our life. It's impossible to know which ones speak to each reader, but it is possible to highlight those teachings that speak to most of us about the ways we choose to make our way in life.

"This Is the Teaching"

There are countless lessons we learn in sacred texts, but every faith tradition has a Golden Rule. Sometimes it is part of secular teachings or wisdom handed down from beloved members of our family, whose familiar lessons originated in a verse from sacred teachings. In Judaism, there is more than one Golden Rule. Rabbi Hillel taught in the first century CE, "What is hateful to you, do not do to others" (Babylonian Talmud, *Shabbat* 31a). His mindful lesson is akin to what we have also learned: "Do unto others what you would have them do unto you," and "Do not do unto others what you would not have them do unto you." They are two sides of the same coin. They speak to the relationships we create between us and our neighbors. Further, we learn, "Love your neighbor as yourself," a phrase first found in Leviticus 19:18, as part of the Holiness Code in Torah, but which is also cited in Christian Gospels. Such kernels of biblical wisdom are meant to focus our greatest human effort on the task of building relationships with others in our life. All this is a part of living in covenant with God.

In this time of life when age equals wisdom, it isn't uncommon to be asked what served as a guide for decisions in our life. Upon reflection, some identify parents or grandparents as keen observers of life and marvelous role models. Their adherence to a strict moral code left a deep impression on their family. Some identify mentors and coworkers whose insights into daily work and issues demonstrated how to navigate a complicated and sometimes unkind world. Their perseverance modeled commitment to important goals and values. In the end, all their lessons became a Torah of sorts for us.

Indeed, Torah is more than the Bible. Only by means of the strictest definition is Torah limited to the Five Books of Moses. When the Five Books were translated into Greek, the word *nomos*, meaning "law," was used to describe Torah. But that was a mistake, because the Hebrew word *torah* means "teaching." Torah is filled with laws, but it is also a living document. In effect, anything that teaches about the depth and breadth of Torah is Torah. The books of Prophets are Torah, as are the books of Writings in the Hebrew Bible. Mishnah and Talmud, *Shulchan Aruch*, and other important parts of Jewish literature are Torah. By extrapolation, even the stories of Sholem Aleichem and the movies of Woody Allen are Torahs of sorts, too.

Ultimately, our own insights into life and the ways we chose to keep the covenant with God is Torah, too. Within Torah itself, we read, *V'zot hatorah*, "This is the teaching" (Deuteronomy 4:44). It is an expression that doesn't mean "This is the Torah," but rather what follows is the teaching on a particular subject. Likewise, we have reached a point in our life when our words reflect the legacy of our deeds. Now we have the privilege to put into words what we have done with our hands. It is time to say to our family and friends, *V'zot hatorah*, "This is the teaching as I see it." And even when younger generations appear not to be listening to our sage advice, we know in our own hearts that the long way we have come is by virtue of the sacred teachings we found and in the faith we reached in God.

Each of us possesses a legacy we wish to bequeath to family and friends. When our ancestor Jacob (also known as Israel) was on his deathbed, he was afraid. He didn't fear death itself. He feared the possibility that his faith might die with him. The promise God made him and his father, Isaac, and his father's father, Abraham, was the only real treasure that he could bequeath to his children. His body would be returned to the earth, as we know, "for from dust you came; to dust you shall return" (Genesis 3:19). But what of his faith? Would a nation of Israel be at hand, a future for our people, or would it die with him?

At once, Jacob's sons responded to their father's fear. Together, they said, *Shema Yisrael, Adonai Eloheinu, Adonai Echad*, "Hear, O Israel, the Lord is Our God, too, the Lord is One God." To which Jacob responded and said, *Baruch shem kevod malchuto l'olam va'ed*, "Blessed be God's glorious kingdom forever and ever" (Babylonian Talmud, *Pesachim* 56a).

Jacob's children remained faithful to his tradition, which was a tribute to his memory and the ultimate gift of eternal life they could bestow upon him. His spirit truly lives on. His life's work continues to flourish. There is no greater evidence of its truth than in the multiple generations of Jews that have flourished since those words were uttered. Life does not end with the grave. The soul never dies. When children emulate their parents and grandparents, their loved ones live on through them. Shadow grief can finally fade when we transform it into good deeds.

Abraham and Sarah, Isaac and Rebecca, Jacob and Rachel and Leah all fulfilled their covenant with God. Moses, in his time, brought the Israelite people to a place where they pledged themselves and their children to the covenant, too. When Moses's death was drawing near, the Torah reads, *Hen karvu yamecha lamut*, "Your days are coming to an end" (Deuteronomy 31:14). The Rabbis explain that while Moses and the Israelites were alarmed by the fact that his leadership was ending, they were soon reminded that only Moses's *days*, his physical life, were coming to an end. All that he meant to the Israelites would endure in the ways they honored his legacy, deeds, and ways.

God told Moses to single out Joshua and confer upon him Moses's authority. Joshua would succeed Moses and lead the Israelite people over the Jordan River into the Promised Land. Moses charged Joshua, *Chazak ve'ematz*, "Be strong and resolute: for you shall bring the Israelites into the land that I promised them on oath, and I will be with you" (Deuteronomy 31:23). In Hebrew, *Chazak ve'ematz* remains a profound charge to anyone who is accepting the mantle of leadership. For Moses, this transference of power was a sign of the end of his days but not the end of his influence. For Joshua, it was a sign of the confidence God and Moses identified in him and the responsibility they believed he could bear.

Over years, we gained the confidence it took to bear exceptional responsibilities for family, work, and community. With varying but ultimately increasing faith, we lived up to our personal expectations and to God's. As we contemplate our mortality, we are like Moses, who had to face the reality of the end of his days and who had the privilege to charge his successor with the duties of faith in the future. Like Moses, we would prefer if it could be said of us not only that life was good to us, but also that we were good to life. And, like Moses, we would enjoy the privilege to say to our progeny, *Chazak ve'ematz*, "Be strong and of good courage." Though our days are limited, the far-reaching power of love, deeds, and faith endure in the able hands and hearts of those who live beyond our years.

God of Me

Years ago, I was summoned to the hospital by the family of a man who had lived a long life. He was dying. His days were filled with both prosperity and adversity. He had known joy and sorrow, success and some failure. He was not an overly observant Jewish man, but neither was he without faith in God. He raised his family according to Jewish customs in the synagogue, he celebrated the holidays, and he led his life according to important lessons from Jewish and secular sources over the years. In times of joy, he thanked God. In times of adversity, he sought God as a source of strength and courage. He was not demonstrative in his method; he was private in his prayer and thoughts about God. But now, after months of being in and out of the hospital, he knew that this time was different.

When I entered his hospital room he was sitting up in bed. His wife was standing nearby. When I put my hand on his shoulder, he said to me in a soft voice, "My soul aches." I had never heard these words before, and he had never felt this ache before. It was the kind of ache a man feels only once in his lifetime. Now, he was keenly aware that he was nearing a threshold that would take him from this world to life in the hereafter. What can anyone say to ease the ache this man felt deep in his soul?

The search for God in our life enables us to avail ourselves of blessings and goodness. We strive to preserve these blessings with God's help, too. We seek God's presence and pray for God's graciousness toward us. More than anything we seek peace over the course of a lifetime. Standing with the man and his wife, I said to him in a soft voice, in Hebrew and English, "May God bless you and protect you. May God's countenance shine upon you and be good to you. May God grant you peace." He nodded his head. No more words.

The many years of our life are full. More often than not, we are able to say that it was full with more of what we wanted and needed, and less of what we tried to avoid and overcome. No life is perfect or without regrets, but every life begins with the potential to make God's blessings part of our journey, God's presence part of our experience, and God's hope part of our destination. Our ancestors' relationships with God have become part of the liturgy we recite every day. We honor their place in our history. We thank them for the paths they tread. We stand on their shoulders. It is a heady responsibility we bear if we understand it correctly. When we became adults in the Jewish community, we took on what is known as *ol mitzvot*, "the yoke of the commandments." As soon as we came of age, we instantly became responsible for the commandments our ancestors handed down to us. We would become the next link in a chain of tradition, which, according to some, is only as strong as its weakest link.

Torah is our strength. God, the Giver of Torah, used Torah to redeem our people from Egypt. Ever since, we, like our ancestors, have integrated Torah into our lives from the time we were children. Now, we see that just as God was not always present to us, we were not always present to God. Nevertheless, our image of God has grown and matured even as we have grown and matured. We see that we can imagine God in all the times of our life.

God's love, honor, comfort, and strength are with us all our life. The journey is not always easy, but especially in the transformational times of our life we learn more about ourselves, until, finally, in our later years we discover that blessings have accompanied us along the way.

It is an awesome task to become the link that connects one generation to the next. Not only is a Torah physically heavy, but it is also heavily loaded with the responsibility of ages. For some, it is easier to let others be the link while they walk away from history and duty. For others, thankfully, their hands are strengthened through prayer, study, and deeds. The understanding of their task comes through the doing, just as it has always been for our ancestors before us. The duty comes naturally and the tradition endures.

The privilege to hold fast to Torah comes to us through the merit of our ancestors. They took the first steps and made the sacrifices. They lived in God's presence. They questioned God's role and persevered with God's help. They thanked God for their blessings and sought God's courage when they needed help. The God of our ancestors is our God, too. The God of Abraham, God of Isaac, God of Jacob, God of Sarah, God of Rebecca, God of Rachel, and God of Leah is, after all these years, the God of me.

DISCUSSION GUIDE

The purpose of a discussion guide is to engage you, the reader, in discussion about the subject of the book. As with any Jewish texts, personal study is important but not necessarily enough. Study with a partner or in a group is best. It allows for discussion, analysis, and debate about a shared experience that leads to deeper understanding and greater awareness. On the subject of God and our hope to enjoy a personal relationship with God, all of us need partners with whom to share meaningful and sincere discussion.

As you participate in or lead a group discussion, keep in mind the following:

1) There is no authentic way to believe in God, except to agree that God is only One God, not three, not two, and not none. Many comments about how to imagine One God should be welcomed and respected.

2) By definition, "midrash" means to investigate, inquire, ask, interpret, and even demand something of the Torah text. The Rabbis were predictably traditional when they investigated Torah for meaning, but they were also unpredictably daring. They pushed the boundaries of inquiry to anticipate questions and to provide answers. Encourage discussion that reaches the boundary of meaningful inquiry.

3) While individual conclusions are important, it is also vital to reach some consensus. Because each person enjoys a personal relationship with God, we all share a common covenant with God. In each chapter, identify personal and universal Jewish lessons.

4) Many groups and leaders will emerge to take up the subject of this book and the texts within it. Consider one leader to guide the discussion of the whole book or one leader to guide the discussion of each chapter. Or consider the manner that suits your readers' group, classroom, or adult education setting so that the God of you can be discovered and imagined for a lifetime.

The following study guide is organized around each chapter—its Torah text and midrash commentary. You'll recognize the full Torah text and midrash. Following the texts, you will find questions to guide you through thoughtful discussions about the texts and their implications. By no means should you consider these questions or guidelines adequate to cover the full subject of the book. Rather, they are a means to further discussion that might reflect the unique makeup of your group. Let the purpose of the book lead you to new boundaries of discovery about the One God and the ways you can imagine God, today and tomorrow.

Chapter 1
God Is Everywhere

Torah Text: *Exodus 3:1–4*
Rabbinic Text: *Exodus Rabbah 11:5*

Torah

Now Moses, tending the flock of his father-in-law, Jethro ... drove the flock into the wilderness, and came to Horeb, the mountain of God. An angel of the Lord appeared to him in a blazing fire out of a bush. He gazed, and there was a bush all aflame, yet the bush was not consumed. Moses said, "I must turn aside to look at this marvelous sight; why doesn't the bush burn up?" When the Lord saw that he had turned aside to look, God called to him out of the bush: "Moses! Moses!" He answered, "Here I am."

Midrash

1) According to the Rabbis, why was a bush (or, as described in midrash, thorn bush) an unlikely place for God to appear?
2) In what kind of place do we mistakenly expect God to appear?
3) On the verse including the words "out of the thorn bush" (Exodus 3:4), the Rabbis taught the following about God in a midrash:

A heathen once asked Rabbi Joshua ben Korchah: "Why did God choose a thorn bush from which to speak to Moses?" He replied, "Were it a carob tree or a sycamore tree, you would have asked the same question; but to dismiss you without any reply is not right, so I will tell you why. To teach you that no place is devoid of God's presence, not even a thorn bush."

    a) What do we know about the appearance of a carob or sycamore tree compared to a thorn bush?
    b) How does the midrash explain why God appeared in the middle of a thorn bush?
4) What do the Rabbis want to teach us through this midrash about God's place in our own life? At what times in our life?
5) Looking back in time, when could you have benefited from this lesson about God's presence?
6) How will the midrash help you understand God's presence in the future?

Chapter 2
God Loves Me

Torah Text: *Exodus 32:1–8*
Rabbinic Text: *Pesikta d'Rav Kahana* 128b

Torah

When the people saw that Moses was so long in coming down from [Mount Sinai], the people gathered against Aaron and said to him, "Come, make us a god who shall go before us, for that man Moses, who brought us from the land of Egypt, we do not know what has happened to him." Aaron said to them, "Take off the gold rings that are on the ears of your wives, your sons, and your daughters, and bring them to me." And all the people took off the gold rings that were in their ears and brought them to Aaron. This he took from them and cast in a mold, and made it into a molten calf. And they exclaimed, "This is your god, O Israel, who brought you out of the land of Egypt!" When Aaron saw this, he built an altar before it; and Aaron announced: "Tomorrow shall be a festival of the Lord!" Early next day, the people offered up burnt offerings and brought sacrifices of well-being; they sat down to eat and drink, and then rose to dance.

The Lord spoke to Moses, "Hurry down, for your people, whom you brought out of the land of Egypt, have acted basely. They have been quick to turn aside from the way that I enjoined upon them. They have made themselves a molten calf and bowed low to it and sacrificed to it, saying: 'This is your god, O Israel, who brought you out of the land of Egypt!'"

Midrash

1) When God originally sent Moses to lead the Israelites out of Egypt, God said, "Tell Pharaoh, 'Let My people go!'" What is the difficulty in this text from Exodus 32 that the Rabbis wanted to resolve?

2) Comparing the two verses from Exodus, when do the Israelites "belong" to God?

3) Concerning the difficulty raised by these verses in Exodus, the Rabbis taught the following by way of a parable in midrash:

Rabbi Berechiah, in the name of Rabbi Levi, said: A king had a vine-yard that he entrusted to a tenant. When the wine was good, he said, "How good is the wine of my vineyard." When it was bad, he said, "How bad is the tenant's wine." The tenant said, "Be the wine bad or good, it is yours." So, at first, God said to Moses, "I will send you to Pharaoh that he may let My people go." But after the making of the Golden Calf, God said, "Go, get down, for your people have cor-rupted themselves." Moses said, "So then, when they sin, they are mine; when they are virtuous, they are Yours. Not so, be they sinful or virtuous, they are Yours."

   a) Discuss the parable in these terms:

   God = king
   Moses = tenant
   Israelites = wine

To what other contemporary people or things can you equate God, Moses, and the Israelites to complete the parable?

   b) What is the parable supposed to help us understand about God's covenant with the Israelite people and with us?
4) How does the midrash help you restore your own covenant with God?

Chapter 3

God Lives with Me

Torah Text: *Genesis 12:1–3*
Rabbinic Text: *Genesis Rabbah 39:9*

Torah

The Lord said to Abram, "Go forth from your native land, and from your father's house to the land that I will show you.... I will make of you a great nation, and I will bless you; I will make your name great, and you shall be a blessing. I will bless those who bless you and curse him that curses you; and all the families of the earth shall bless themselves by you."

1) What would have been a faster way to tell Abraham to leave everything behind?
2) Is the Torah being long-winded, or is there something to learn from the detail? What can we understand from the following parts of the verse "Go forth from your ..."?
   a) Land
   b) Birthplace
   c) Father's house
3) How would you imagine Abraham's feelings after being ordered to leave? What would be among his chief concerns?
4) Where in the verse do we find a clue about Abraham's destiny? What specific information is missing, and why?

Midrash

Why didn't God reveal the land to Abraham there and then? In order to make it more beloved in his eyes and to reward him for every step he took [in the direction of Mount Moriah].

1) What evidence is there in the midrash that God wanted Abraham to succeed in reaching Mount Moriah?
2) How does the term "delayed gratification" describe the journey Abraham is taking?
3) How does "delayed gratification" describe your journey and the relationship you can enjoy with God?

Chapter 4
God Teaches Me

Torah Text: *Genesis 11:1–9*
Rabbinic Text: *Midrash Tanchuma, Noach* 18

Torah

Everyone on earth had the same language and the same words.... They said to one another, "Come, let us make bricks and … build us a city, and a tower with its top in the sky, to make a name for our-selves; else we shall be scattered all over the world." The Lord came down to look at the city and tower that man had built, and the Lord said, "If, as one people with one language, this is how they have begun to act, then nothing that they may propose to do will be out of their reach. Let us, then, go down and confound their speech there, so that they shall not understand one another's speech." Thus the Lord scattered them from there over the face of the whole earth; and they stopped building the city. That is why it was called Babel, because the Lord confounded the speech of the whole earth.

1) Rabbinic tradition taught that God is all-powerful (omnipotent), all-knowing (omniscient), and all-present (omnipresent). How does this text challenge these beliefs? Identify the specific part of the text that contains the difficulty.

Midrash

It is only to teach God's creations [human beings], that God did not pass judgment or come to a conclusion until God saw firsthand.

1) What does the midrash give God permission to do, and why?
2) How does the midrash create intimacy between God and God's creations?
3) What other examples can you give to describe how God teaches human beings?

Chapter 5
God Hears Me

Torah Text: *Leviticus 22:17–22*
Rabbinic Text: *Leviticus Rabbah 11:5*

Torah

The Lord spoke to Moses, saying: Speak to Aaron and his sons, and to all the Israelite people, and say to them: When any man of the house of Israel or of the strangers in Israel presents a burnt offering as his offering for any of the votive or any of the freewill offerings that they offer to the Lord, it must, to be acceptable in your favor, be a male without blemish, from cattle or sheep or goats. You shall not offer any that has a defect, for it will not be accepted in your favor. Anything blind, or injured, or maimed, or with a wen [cyst], boil-scar, or scurvy—such you shall not offer to the Lord.

1) Torah is clear about what should and should not be brought to God as an offering. When the Temple was destroyed in 70 CE, prayer replaced sacrifices. What words in the Torah text help you understand the kinds of prayers, words, and meditations you should offer God when you worship today?

Midrash

Rabbi Nehemiah expounded the verse as referring to Moses. When he approached God with special courtesy, God treated him with special courtesy; when he came to God with frankness, God answered him with frankness; when he approached God with lack of directness, God countered him with lack of directness; when he sought a clear statement regarding his affairs, God made clear his affairs for him. (Leviticus Rabbah 11:5)

1) The midrash describes the ways God and Moses responded to each other's words and petitions. How does your own prayer reflect the "response" or feeling you expect when you worship?
2) How does *kavanah* help you prepare for sincere worship?
3) What role does *keva* play in worship for you?
4) What mix of *keva* and *kavanah* is right for you, and when?

Chapter 6
God Knows Me

Torah Text: *Exodus 28:1–3*
Rabbinic Text: *Exodus Rabbah 37:2*

Torah

You shall bring forward your brother Aaron, with his sons, from among the Israelites, to serve Me as priests: Aaron, Nadab and Abihu, Eleazar and Ithamar, the sons of Aaron. Make sacral vestments for your brother Aaron, for dignity and adornment. Next you shall instruct all who are skillful, whom I have endowed with the gift of skill, to make Aaron's vestments, for consecrating him to serve Me as priest.

Midrash

The Sages said: When Moses descended from Sinai and beheld Israel engaged in that unspeakable act, he looked at Aaron, who was beating the Calf with a hammer. The intention of Aaron was really to restrain the people until Moses came down, but Moses thought that Aaron was a partner in their crime and he was incensed against him. Whereupon God said to Moses, "I know that Aaron's intention was quite good."

1) Separating deeds from intentions is a matter of some divine skill. Why is the distinction between the two critical to our relationship between us and other people, and between us and God?
2) What do you believe about Aaron's participation in the incident of the Golden Calf?
3) Accepting the point of this midrash, what can you learn about your role in complicated or misunderstood events?
4) Even if God understands your intentions, what responsibility do you think you have to improve relations with someone who doesn't?

Chapter 7
God Honors Me

Torah Text: *Leviticus 9:1–3, 5–6*
Rabbinic Text: *Leviticus Rabbah 7:2*

Torah

On the eighth day, Moses called Aaron and his sons, and the elders of Israel. He said to Aaron, "Take a calf of the herd for a sin offering and a ram for a burnt offering, without blemish, and bring them before the Lord." They brought to the front of the Tent of Meeting the things that Moses had commanded, and the whole community came forward and stood before the Lord. Moses said, "This is what the Lord has commanded that you do, that the Presence of the Lord may appear to you."

1) Describe the quality of the sacrifice that was brought for an offering? What does "without blemish" suggest to you?
2) Why is the one who offers the animal also the one who decides whether or not it is without blemish?

Midrash

Rabbi Abba ben Yudan said, "All that God has declared to be unclean in animals He has pronounced desirable [*kasher*] in men. In animals He has declared blind or broken or maimed or having a wen to be unserviceable, but in men He has declared the broken and crushed heart to be desirable." Rabbi Alexandri said, "If a private person uses broken vessels, it is a disgrace to him, but God uses broken vessels, as it is said, 'The Lord is close to the brokenhearted; those crushed in spirit God delivers' (Psalm 34:19); 'I dwell on high, in holiness; yet with the contrite and the lowly in spirit, reviving the spirits of the lowly, reviving the hearts of the contrite' (Isaiah 57:15); 'God heals their broken hearts and binds up their wounds'" (Psalm 147:3).

1) *Kasher* means desirable or fit for use. How does the use of the term *kasher* in the midrash help you understand the role of every human being in God's covenant?
2) What kinds of human brokenness do you observe in others and yourself?

3) How does the midrash change your opinion of others and yourself?

4) The midrash teaches that God uses broken vessels. What examples can you give to illustrate this lesson?

5) We have been taught to honor God. How does this midrash help you understand that God honors you?

6) The psalm teaches us that God heals our "broken hearts and binds up [our] wounds" (Psalm 147:3). When God honors you, how does it contribute to your sense of healing and wholeness?

7) In what new ways are you prepared to see your brokenness or others' as worthy to bring before God?

Chapter 8
God Receives Me

Torah Text: *Jeremiah 3:1, 3:22*
Rabbinic Text: *Pesikta Rabbati* 184a

Torah

[The word of the Lord came to me] as follows: If a man divorces his wife, and she leaves him and marries another man, can he ever go back to her? Would not such a land be defiled? Now you have whored with many lovers: can you return to Me?—says the Lord … Turn back, O rebellious children, I will heal your afflictions!

1) Jeremiah's prophecy describes a covenant between God and Israel that is unique. What words would you use to describe the potential in this covenant?

Midrash

But God is not so. Even though Israel has deserted *Adonai*, and served other gods, God says, "Return unto me, repent and I will receive you." So Jeremiah, too, applies the same contrast, and says, "Though you have played the harlot with many lovers yet return again to me and I will receive you."

1) Over time, what has stood in the way of a relationship between God and you?
2) What difference does God's unconditional love make to you and the relationship that is still available to you?
3) As in any relationship that has been challenged, what will you do differently now as you rebuild your image of God?
4) Jeremiah referred to exile of the people but also of their spirit. How would you compare your own sense of exile from God and the hope for return?
5) What do you need from God at this stage in your life?

Chapter 9
God Comforts Me

Torah Text: *Genesis 17:9–12*
Rabbinic Text: *Genesis Rabbah 48:9*

Torah

As for you, you and your offspring to come throughout the ages shall keep My covenant. Such shall be the covenant between Me and you and your offspring to follow which you shall keep: every male among you shall be circumcised. You shall circumcise the flesh of your foreskin, and that shall be the sign of the covenant between Me and you. And throughout the generations, every male among you shall be circumcised at the age of eight days.

1) In what ways have you felt commanded by God to perform ritual or ethical deeds?
2) How do ancient rites such as circumcision reflect your image of God and the covenant God makes with you?

Midrash

Abraham complained, "Before I was circumcised travelers used to visit me; now that I am circumcised they will no longer visit me?" Said God to Abraham, "Before this, uncircumcised mortals visited you; but now I and My retinue will appear to you." Thus, "And he lifted up his eyes and looked," he saw the *Shechinah* [divine presence] and saw the angels.

1) When did you feel that you served God through the performance of a commandment? Did you feel that God served you, too? How so?
2) What does it mean to you that God replied to Abraham's complaint?
3) How does God as comforter change your image of God?
4) We are taught that God is the source of everything we need. What have you needed from God? What do you think you can expect from God in the future?
5) God did not ignore Abraham's plea. In what way do you believe God might respond to your plea?

Chapter 10
God Strengthens Me

Torah Text: *Exodus 15:11–13*
Rabbinic Text: *Mechilta d'Rabbi Ishmael,* Tractate *Shirata* 5:2

Torah

Who is like You, O Lord, among the celestials;

Who is like You, majestic in holiness,

Awesome in splendor, working wonders!

You put out Your right hand,

The earth swallowed them.

In Your love You lead the people You redeemed;

In Your strength You guide them to Your holy abode.

Midrash

For the sake of the Torah that they were destined to receive, for "Your strength" here is but a designation for the Torah, as in the passage, "The Lord will give strength unto [God's] people" (Psalm 29:11).

1) Torah is God's strength. God gave Torah to the Israelite people. In what way(s) is Torah a source of strength to you? When?
2) At what time in your life did you recognize Torah as a source of strength in your life? What changed?
3) Many sources of strength exist in our life. What makes Torah unique?
4) God gave Torah to the Israelite people and to us. To whom will you give Torah? How will you do it?

Additional Questions for Discussion

1) When you imagine God over your lifetime, what enduring image of God would you like to hold on to?

2) Looking back on childhood, what thoughts about God did you have, revisit, or revise?

3) What lessons about God did you learn in midrash that help you gain insight into stages in your life? Which lessons and which stages?

4) End of life is something everyone must contemplate at some point. What do you think Judaism teaches you about God's presence throughout your life?

5) In chapter 10, the elderly man whom I visited in the hospital said to me, "My soul aches." What does his remark mean to you?

6) What is your opinion of the Rabbis' midrash lessons? Were they daring? Were they insightful? Did they go far enough to challenge or awaken your understanding of God?

7) Is there a Torah text you would call your favorite? Why? What has it taught you in your lifetime?

8) The end of every Jewish lesson should prompt the question, what will I learn next? How would you answer that question for yourself?

Notes

1. Ernest Kurtz and Katherine Ketcham, *The Spirituality of Imperfection* (New York: Bantam Press, 1993), 15.

2. *The Penguin Book of Hebrew Verse*, ed. and trans. T. Carmi (New York: Penguin Books, 1981), 419.

3. David Polish, "History as the Source of the Mitzvah," in *Gates of Mitzvah*, ed. Simeon J. Maslin (New York: CCAR Press, 1979), 104.

4. Bruce Horacek, "A Heurisitc Model of Grieving after High-Grief Deaths," *Death Studies* 19, no. 1 (January 1995): 21–31.

5. Dov Peretz Elkins, ed., *Moments of Transcendence: A Devotional Commentary on the High Holiday Mahzor*, vol. 2, *Yom Kippur* (Growth Assoc., 1990).

6. Ibid.

Suggestions for Further Reading

Brown, Erica. *Spiritual Boredom: Rediscovering the Wonder of Judaism.* Woodstock, VT: Jewish Lights Publishing, 2009.

Cohen, Norman. *Voices from Genesis: Guiding Us through the Stages of Life.* Woodstock, VT: Jewish Lights Publishing, 2001.

———. *The Way Into Torah.* Woodstock, VT: Jewish Lights Publishing, 2000.

Comins, Mike. *Making Prayer Real: Leading Jewish Spiritual Voices on Why Prayer Is Difficult and What to Do about It.* Woodstock, VT: Jewish Lights Publishing, 2010.

Gilman, Neil. *Traces of God: Seeing God in Torah, History and Everyday Life.* Woodstock, VT: Jewish Lights Publishing, 2008.

———. *The Way Into Encountering God in Judaism.* Woodstock, VT: Jewish Lights Publishing, 2004.

Gittlesohn, Roland B. "Mitzvah without Miracles." In *Gates of Mitzvah,* edited by Simeon J. Maslin, 108–110. New York: CCAR Press, 1986.

Green, Arthur. *Radical Judaism: Rethinking God and Tradition.* New Haven, CT: Yale University Press, 2010.

Hoffman, Lawrence A. *The Way Into Jewish Prayer.* Woodstock, VT: Jewish Lights Publishing, 2000.

Korngold, Jamie. *The God Upgrade: Finding Your 21st-Century Spirituality in Judaism's 5,000-Year-Old Tradition.* Woodstock, VT: Jewish Lights Publishing, 2011.

Kushner, Harold. *Who Needs God.* New York: Fireside, 2002.

Kushner, Lawrence. *God Was in This Place & I, i Did Not Know.* Woodstock, VT: Jewish Lights Publishing, 1993.

Lelyveld, Arthur J. "Mitzvah: The Larger Context." In *Gates of Mitzvah,* edited by Simeon J. Maslin, 111–115. New York: CCAR Press, 1986.

Schaalman, Herman. "The Divine Authority of Mitzvah." In *Gates of Mitzvah,* edited by Simeon J. Maslin, 100–103. New York: CCAR Press, 1986.

Schulweis, Harold. *For Those Who Can't Believe: Overcoming Obstacles to Faith.* New York: Harper Perennial, 1995.

Silver, Abba Hillel. *Where Judaism Differs: An Inquiry into the Distinctiveness of Judaism.* New York: Collier Books, 1987.

Steinberg, Milton. *Basic Judaism.* New York: A Harvest/HBJ Book, 1975.

Wolpe, David. *Why Faith Matters.* New York: HarperOne, 2008.

Bar/Bat Mitzvah

The JGirl's Guide: The Young Jewish Woman's Handbook for Coming of Age *By Penina Adelman, Ali Feldman and Shulamit Reinharz* This inspirational, interactive guidebook helps pre-teen Jewish girls address the many issues surrounding coming of age. 6 x 9, 240 pp, Quality PB, 978-1-58023-215-9 **$14.99** *For ages 11 & up*
Also Available: **The JGirl's Teacher's and Parent's Guide**
8½ x 11, 56 pp, PB, 978-1-58023-225-8 **$8.99**

Bar/Bat Mitzvah Basics, 2nd Edition: A Practical Family Guide to Coming of Age Together *Edited by Helen Leneman; Foreword by Rabbi Jeffrey K. Salkin*
6 x 9, 240 pp, Quality PB, 978-1-58023-151-0 **$18.95**

The Bar/Bat Mitzvah Memory Book, 2nd Edition: An Album for Treasuring the Spiritual Celebration *By Rabbi Jeffrey K. Salkin and Nina Salkin*
8 x 10, 48 pp, 2-color text, Deluxe HC, ribbon marker, 978-1-58023-263-0 **$19.99**

For Kids—Putting God on Your Guest List, 2nd Edition: How to Claim the Spiritual Meaning of Your Bar or Bat Mitzvah *By Rabbi Jeffrey K. Salkin*
6 x 9, 144 pp, Quality PB, 978-1-58023-308-8 **$15.99** *For ages 11–13*

Putting God on the Guest List, 3rd Edition: How to Reclaim the Spiritual Meaning of Your Child's Bar or Bat Mitzvah *By Rabbi Jeffrey K. Salkin*
6 x 9, 224 pp, Quality PB, 978-1-58023-222-7 **$16.99**; HC, 978-1-58023-260-9 **$24.99**
Also Available: **Putting God on the Guest List Teacher's Guide**
8½ x 11, 48 pp, PB, 978-1-58023-226-5 **$8.99**

Tough Questions Jews Ask: A Young Adult's Guide to Building a Jewish Life *By Rabbi Edward Feinstein* 6 x 9, 160 pp, Quality PB, 978-1-58023-139-8 **$14.99** *For ages 11 & up*
Also Available: **Tough Questions Jews Ask Teacher's Guide**
8½ x 11, 72 pp, PB, 978-1-58023-187-9 **$8.95**

Bible Study/Midrash

The Modern Men's Torah Commentary: New Insights from Jewish Men on the 54 Weekly Torah Portions *Edited by Rabbi Jeffrey K. Salkin* A major contribution to modern biblical commentary. Addresses the most important concerns of modern men by opening them up to the messages of Torah.
6 x 9, 368 pp, HC, 978-1-58023-395-8 **$24.99**

The Genesis of Leadership: What the Bible Teaches Us about Vision, Values and Leading Change *By Rabbi Nathan Laufer; Foreword by Senator Joseph I. Lieberman*
6 x 9, 288 pp, Quality PB, 978-1-58023-352-1 **$18.99**

Hineini in Our Lives: Learning How to Respond to Others through 14 Biblical Texts and Personal Stories *By Rabbi Norman J. Cohen, PhD* 6 x 9, 240 pp, Quality PB, 978-1-58023-274-6 **$16.99**

A Man's Responsibility: A Jewish Guide to Being a Son, a Partner in Marriage, a Father and a Community Leader *By Rabbi Joseph B. Meszler*
6 x 9, 192 pp, Quality PB, 978-1-58023-435-1 **$16.99**; HC, 978-1-58023-362-0 **$21.99**

Moses and the Journey to Leadership: Timeless Lessons of Effective Management from the Bible and Today's Leaders *By Rabbi Norman J. Cohen, PhD*
6 x 9, 240 pp, Quality PB, 978-1-58023-351-4 **$18.99**; HC, 978-1-58023-227-2 **$21.99**

Righteous Gentiles in the Hebrew Bible: Ancient Role Models for Sacred Relationships *By Rabbi Jeffrey K. Salkin; Foreword by Rabbi Harold M. Schulweis; Preface by Phyllis Tickle* 6 x 9, 192 pp, Quality PB, 978-1-58023-364-4 **$18.99**

The Triumph of Eve & Other Subversive Bible Tales *By Matt Biers-Ariel* 5½ x 8½, 192 pp, Quality PB, 978-1-59473-176-1 **$14.99** *(A book from SkyLight Paths, Jewish Lights' sister imprint)*

The Wisdom of Judaism: An Introduction to the Values of the Talmud *By Rabbi Dov Peretz Elkins* 6 x 9, 192 pp, Quality PB, 978-1-58023-327-9 **$16.99**
Also Available: **The Wisdom of Judaism Teacher's Guide**
8½ x 11, 18 pp, PB, 978-1-58023-350-7 **$8.99**

Holidays/Holy Days

Who by Fire, Who by Water—Un'taneh Tokef

Edited by Rabbi Lawrence A. Hoffman, PhD

Examines the prayer's theology, authorship and poetry through a set of lively essays, all written in accessible language.

6 x 9, 272 pp, HC, 978-1-58023-424-5 **$24.99**

Rosh Hashanah Readings: Inspiration, Information and Contemplation
Yom Kippur Readings: Inspiration, Information and Contemplation

Edited by Rabbi Dov Peretz Elkins; Section Introductions from Arthur Green's These Are the Words

An extraordinary collection of readings, prayers and insights that will enable you to enter into the spirit of the High Holy Days in a personal and powerful way, permitting the meaning of the Jewish New Year to enter the heart.

Rosh Hashanah: 6 x 9, 400 pp, Quality PB, 978-1-58023-437-5 **$19.99**; HC, 978-1-58023-239-5 **$24.99**
Yom Kippur: 6 x 9, 368 pp, Quality PB, 978-1-58023-438-2 **$19.99**; HC, 978-1-58023-271-5 **$24.99**

Jewish Holidays: A Brief Introduction for Christians
By Rabbi Kerry M. Olitzky and Rabbi Daniel Judson
5½ x 8½, 176 pp, Quality PB, 978-1-58023-302-6 **$16.99**

Reclaiming Judaism as a Spiritual Practice: Holy Days and Shabbat
By Rabbi Goldie Milgram 7 x 9, 272 pp, Quality PB, 978-1-58023-205-0 **$19.99**

7th Heaven: Celebrating Shabbat with Rebbe Nachman of Breslov
By Moshe Mykoff with the Breslov Research Institute
5⅛ x 8¼, 224 pp, Deluxe PB w/ flaps, 978-1-58023-175-6 **$18.95**

Shabbat, 2nd Edition: The Family Guide to Preparing for and Celebrating
the Sabbath *By Dr. Ron Wolfson*
7 x 9, 320 pp, Illus., Quality PB, 978-1-58023-164-0 **$19.99**

Hanukkah, 2nd Edition: The Family Guide to Spiritual Celebration
By Dr. Ron Wolfson 7 x 9, 240 pp, Illus., Quality PB, 978-1-58023-122-0 **$18.95**

The Jewish Family Fun Book, 2nd Edition: Holiday Projects, Everyday Activities,
and Travel Ideas with Jewish Themes *By Danielle Dardashti and Roni Sarig; Illus. by Avi Katz*
6 x 9, 304 pp, 70+ b/w illus. & diagrams, Quality PB, 978-1-58023-333-0 **$18.99**

The Jewish Lights Book of Fun Classroom Activities: Simple and Seasonal
Projects for Teachers and Students *By Danielle Dardashti and Roni Sarig*
6 x 9, 240 pp, Quality PB, 978-1-58023-206-7 **$19.99**

Passover

My People's Passover Haggadah
Traditional Texts, Modern Commentaries

Edited by Rabbi Lawrence A. Hoffman, PhD, and David Arnow, PhD

A diverse and exciting collection of commentaries on the traditional Passover Haggadah—in two volumes!

Vol. 1: 7 x 10, 304 pp, HC, 978-1-58023-354-5 **$24.99**
Vol. 2: 7 x 10, 320 pp, HC, 978-1-58023-346-0 **$24.99**

Leading the Passover Journey: The Seder's Meaning Revealed,
the Haggadah's Story Retold *By Rabbi Nathan Laufer*
Uncovers the hidden meaning of the Seder's rituals and customs.
6 x 9, 224 pp, Quality PB, 978-1-58023-399-6 **$18.99**; HC, 978-1-58023-211-1 **$24.99**

The Women's Passover Companion: Women's Reflections on the Festival of Freedom
Edited by Rabbi Sharon Cohen Anisfeld, Tara Mohr and Catherine Spector; Foreword by Paula E. Hyman
6 x 9, 352 pp, Quality PB, 978-1-58023-231-9 **$19.99**; HC, 978-1-58023-128-2 **$24.95**

The Women's Seder Sourcebook: Rituals & Readings for Use at the Passover Seder
Edited by Rabbi Sharon Cohen Anisfeld, Tara Mohr and Catherine Spector
6 x 9, 384 pp, Quality PB, 978-1-58023-232-6 **$19.99**

Creating Lively Passover Seders: A Sourcebook of Engaging Tales, Texts & Activities
By David Arnow, PhD 7 x 9, 416 pp, Quality PB, 978-1-58023-184-8 **$24.99**

Passover, 2nd Edition: The Family Guide to Spiritual Celebration
By Dr. Ron Wolfson with Joel Lurie Grishaver 7 x 9, 416 pp, Quality PB, 978-1-58023-174-9 **$19.95**

Life Cycle

Marriage/Parenting/Family/Aging

The New Jewish Baby Album: Creating and Celebrating the Beginning of a Spiritual Life—A Jewish Lights Companion
By the Editors at Jewish Lights; Foreword by Anita Diamant; Preface by Rabbi Sandy Eisenberg Sasso
A spiritual keepsake that will be treasured for generations. More than just a memory book, *shows you how—and why it's important*—to create a Jewish home and a Jewish life. 8 x 10, 64 pp, Deluxe Padded HC, Full-color illus., 978-1-58023-138-1 **$19.95**

The Jewish Pregnancy Book: A Resource for the Soul, Body & Mind during Pregnancy, Birth & the First Three Months *By Sandy Falk, MD, and Rabbi Daniel Judson, with Steven A. Rapp* Medical information, prayers and rituals for each stage of pregnancy. 7 x 10, 208 pp, b/w photos, Quality PB, 978-1-58023-178-7 **$16.95**

Celebrating Your New Jewish Daughter: Creating Jewish Ways to Welcome Baby Girls into the Covenant—New and Traditional Ceremonies *By Debra Nussbaum Cohen; Foreword by Rabbi Sandy Eisenberg Sasso* 6 x 9, 272 pp, Quality PB, 978-1-58023-090-2 **$18.95**

The New Jewish Baby Book, 2nd Edition: Names, Ceremonies & Customs—A Guide for Today's Families *By Anita Diamant* 6 x 9, 320 pp, Quality PB, 978-1-58023-251-7 **$19.99**

Parenting as a Spiritual Journey: Deepening Ordinary and Extraordinary Events into Sacred Occasions *By Rabbi Nancy Fuchs-Kreimer, PhD* 6 x 9, 224 pp, Quality PB, 978-1-58023-016-2 **$17.99**

Parenting Jewish Teens: A Guide for the Perplexed
By Joanne Doades Explores the questions and issues that shape the world in which today's Jewish teenagers live and offers constructive advice to parents.
6 x 9, 176 pp, Quality PB, 978-1-58023-305-7 **$16.99**

Judaism for Two: A Spiritual Guide for Strengthening and Celebrating Your Loving Relationship *By Rabbi Nancy Fuchs-Kreimer, PhD, and Rabbi Nancy H. Wiener, DMin; Foreword by Rabbi Elliot N. Dorff, PhD*
Addresses the ways Jewish teachings can enhance and strengthen committed relationships. 6 x 9, 224 pp, Quality PB, 978-1-58023-254-8 **$16.99**

The Creative Jewish Wedding Book, 2nd Edition: A Hands-On Guide to New & Old Traditions, Ceremonies & Celebrations *By Gabrielle Kaplan-Mayer*
9 x 9, 288 pp, b/w photos, Quality PB, 978-1-58023-398-9 **$19.99**

Divorce Is a Mitzvah: A Practical Guide to Finding Wholeness and Holiness When Your Marriage Dies *By Rabbi Perry Netter; Afterword by Rabbi Laura Geller*
6 x 9, 224 pp, Quality PB, 978-1-58023-172-5 **$16.95**

Embracing the Covenant: Converts to Judaism Talk About Why & How
By Rabbi Allan Berkowitz and Patti Moskovitz 6 x 9, 192 pp, Quality PB, 978-1-879045-50-7 **$16.95**

The Guide to Jewish Interfaith Family Life: An InterfaithFamily.com Handbook
Edited by Ronnie Friedland and Edmund Case
6 x 9, 384 pp, Quality PB, 978-1-58023-153-4 **$18.95**

A Heart of Wisdom: Making the Jewish Journey from Midlife through the Elder Years
Edited by Susan Berrin; Foreword by Rabbi Harold Kushner
6 x 9, 384 pp, Quality PB, 978-1-58023-051-3 **$18.95**

Introducing My Faith and My Community: The Jewish Outreach Institute Guide for the Christian in a Jewish Interfaith Relationship
By Rabbi Kerry M. Olitzky 6 x 9, 176 pp, Quality PB, 978-1-58023-192-3 **$16.99**

Making a Successful Jewish Interfaith Marriage: The Jewish Outreach Institute Guide to Opportunities, Challenges and Resources *By Rabbi Kerry M. Olitzky with Joan Peterson Littman*
6 x 9, 176 pp, Quality PB, 978-1-58023-170-1 **$16.95**

A Man's Responsibility: A Jewish Guide to Being a Son, a Partner in Marriage, a Father and a Community Leader *By Rabbi Joseph B. Meszler*
6 x 9, 192 pp, Quality PB, 978-1-58023-435-1 **$16.99**; HC, 978-1-58023-362-0 **$21.99**

So That Your Values Live On: Ethical Wills and How to Prepare Them
Edited by Rabbi Jack Riemer and Rabbi Nathaniel Stampfer
6 x 9, 272 pp, Quality PB, 978-1-879045-34-7 **$18.99**

Spirituality/Women's Interest

The Divine Feminine in Biblical Wisdom Literature: Selections Annotated & Explained *Translation & Annotation by Rabbi Rami Shapiro* 5½ x 8½, 240 pp, Quality PB, 978-1-59473-109-9 **$16.99** *(A book from SkyLight Paths, Jewish Lights' sister imprint)*

The Quotable Jewish Woman: Wisdom, Inspiration & Humor from the Mind & Heart *Edited by Elaine Bernstein Partnow* 6 x 9, 496 pp, Quality PB, 978-1-58023-236-4 **$19.99**

The Women's Haftarah Commentary: New Insights from Women Rabbis on the 54 Weekly Haftarah Portions, the 5 Megillot & Special Shabbatot *Edited by Rabbi Elyse Goldstein* 6 x 9, 560 pp, Quality PB, 978-1-58023-371-2 **$19.99**

The Women's Torah Commentary: New Insights from Women Rabbis on the 54 Weekly Torah Portions *Edited by Rabbi Elyse Goldstein* 6 x 9, 496 pp, Quality PB, 978-1-58023-370-5 **$19.99**; HC, 978-1-58023-076-6 **$34.95**

New Jewish Feminism: Probing the Past, Forging the Future *Edited by Rabbi Elyse Goldstein; Foreword by Anita Diamant* 6 x 9, 480 pp, HC, 978-1-58023-359-0 **$24.99**

Spirituality/Crafts
(from SkyLight Paths, Jewish Lights' sister imprint)

Beading—The Creative Spirit: Finding Your Sacred Center through the Art of Beadwork *By Wendy Ellsworth*
Invites you on a spiritual pilgrimage into the kaleidoscope world of glass and color.
7 x 9, 240 pp, 8-page full-color insert, b/w photos and diagrams, Quality PB, 978-1-59473-267-6 **$18.99**

Contemplative Crochet: A Hands-On Guide for Interlocking Faith and Craft *By Cindy Crandall-Frazier; Foreword by Linda Skolnik*
Will take you on a path deeper into your crocheting and your spiritual awareness.
7 x 9, 208 pp, b/w photos, Quality PB, 978-1-59473-238-6 **$16.99**

The Knitting Way: A Guide to Spiritual Self-Discovery *By Linda Skolnik and Janice MacDaniels* Shows how to use knitting to strengthen your spiritual self. 7 x 9, 240 pp, b/w photos, Quality PB, 978-1-59473-079-5 **$16.99**

The Painting Path: Embodying Spiritual Discovery through Yoga, Brush and Color *By Linda Novick; Foreword by Richard Segalman*
Explores the divine connection you can experience through art.
7 x 9, 208 pp, 8-page full-color insert, b/w photos, Quality PB, 978-1-59473-226-3 **$18.99**

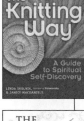

The Quilting Path: A Guide to Spiritual Self-Discovery through Fabric, Thread and Kabbalah *By Louise Silk* Explores how to cultivate personal growth through quilt making. 7 x 9, 192 pp, b/w photos, Quality PB, 978-1-59473-206-5 **$16.99**

The Scrapbooking Journey: A Hands-On Guide to Spiritual Discovery *By Cory Richardson-Lauve; Foreword by Stacy Julian*
Reveals how this craft can become a practice used to deepen and shape your life.
7 x 9, 176 pp, 8-page full-color insert, b/w photos, Quality PB, 978-1-59473-216-4 **$18.99**

Travel

Israel—A Spiritual Travel Guide, 2nd Edition: A Companion for the Modern Jewish Pilgrim *By Rabbi Lawrence A. Hoffman, PhD* 4¾ x 10, 256 pp, Illus., Quality PB, 978-1-58023-261-6 **$18.99**
Also Available: **The Israel Mission Leader's Guide** 5½ x 8½, 16 pp, PB, 978-1-58023-085-8 **$4.95**

Twelve Steps

100 Blessings Every Day: Daily Twelve Step Recovery Affirmations, Exercises for Personal Growth & Renewal Reflecting Seasons of the Jewish Year *By Rabbi Kerry M. Olitzky; Foreword by Rabbi Neil Gillman, PhD* 4½ x 6½, 432 pp, Quality PB, 978-1-879045-30-9 **$16.99**

Recovery from Codependence: A Jewish Twelve Steps Guide to Healing Your Soul *By Rabbi Kerry M. Olitzky* 6 x 9, 160 pp, Quality PB, 978-1-879045-32-3 **$13.95**

Twelve Jewish Steps to Recovery, 2nd Edition: A Personal Guide to Turning from Alcoholism & Other Addictions—Drugs, Food, Gambling, Sex...
By Rabbi Kerry M. Olitzky and Stuart A. Copans, MD; Preface by Abraham J. Twerski, MD
6 x 9, 160 pp, Quality PB, 978-1-58023-409-2 **$16.99**

Theology/Philosophy/The Way Into... Series

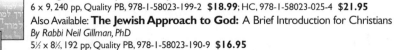

The Way Into... series offers an accessible and highly usable "guided tour" of the Jewish faith, people, history and beliefs—in total, an introduction to Judaism that will enable you to understand and interact with the sacred texts of the Jewish tradition. Each volume is written by a leading contemporary scholar and teacher, and explores one key aspect of Judaism. The Way Into... series enables all readers to achieve a real sense of Jewish cultural literacy through guided study.

The Way Into Encountering God in Judaism
By Rabbi Neil Gillman, PhD
For everyone who wants to understand how Jews have encountered God throughout history and today.
6 x 9, 240 pp, Quality PB, 978-1-58023-199-2 **$18.99**; HC, 978-1-58023-025-4 **$21.95**
Also Available: **The Jewish Approach to God:** A Brief Introduction for Christians
By Rabbi Neil Gillman, PhD
5½ x 8½, 192 pp, Quality PB, 978-1-58023-190-9 **$16.95**

The Way Into Jewish Mystical Tradition
By Rabbi Lawrence Kushner
Allows readers to interact directly with the sacred mystical texts of the Jewish tradition. An accessible introduction to the concepts of Jewish mysticism, their religious and spiritual significance, and how they relate to life today.
6 x 9, 224 pp, Quality PB, 978-1-58023-200-5 **$18.99**; HC, 978-1-58023-029-2 **$21.95**

The Way Into Jewish Prayer
By Rabbi Lawrence A. Hoffman, PhD
Opens the door to 3,000 years of Jewish prayer, making anyone feel at home in the Jewish way of communicating with God.
6 x 9, 208 pp, Quality PB, 978-1-58023-201-2 **$18.99**

Also Available: **The Way Into Jewish Prayer Teacher's Guide**
By Rabbi Jennifer Ossakow Goldsmith
8½ x 11, 42 pp, PB, 978-1-58023-345-3 **$8.99**
Download a free copy at www.jewishlights.com.

The Way Into Judaism and the Environment
By Jeremy Benstein, PhD
Explores the ways in which Judaism contributes to contemporary social-environmental issues, the extent to which Judaism is part of the problem and how it can be part of the solution.
6 x 9, 288 pp, Quality PB, 978-1-58023-368-2 **$18.99**; HC, 978-1-58023-268-5 **$24.99**

The Way Into *Tikkun Olam* (Repairing the World)
By Rabbi Elliot N. Dorff, PhD
An accessible introduction to the Jewish concept of the individual's responsibility to care for others and repair the world.
6 x 9, 304 pp, Quality PB, 978-1-58023-328-6 **$18.99**; 320 pp, HC, 978-1-58023-269-2 **$24.99**

The Way Into Torah
By Rabbi Norman J. Cohen, PhD
Helps guide you in the exploration of the origins and development of Torah, explains why it should be studied and how to do it.
6 x 9, 176 pp, Quality PB, 978-1-58023-198-5 **$16.99**

The Way Into the Varieties of Jewishness
By Sylvia Barack Fishman, PhD
Explores the religious and historical understanding of what it has meant to be Jewish from ancient times to the present controversy over "Who is a Jew?"
6 x 9, 288 pp, Quality PB, 978-1-58023-367-5 **$18.99**; HC, 978-1-58023-030-8 **$24.99**

Theology/Philosophy

Jewish Theology in Our Time: A New Generation Explores the
Foundations and Future of Jewish Belief *Edited by Rabbi Elliot J. Cosgrove, PhD;
Foreword by Rabbi David J. Wolpe; Preface by Rabbi Carole B. Balin, PhD*
A powerful and challenging examination of what Jews can believe—by a new gen-
eration's most dynamic and innovative thinkers.
6 x 9, 240 pp, HC, 978-1-58023-413-9 **$24.99**

Maimonides, Spinoza and Us: Toward an Intellectually Vibrant Judaism
By Rabbi Marc D. Angel, PhD A challenging look at two great Jewish philosophers
and what their thinking means to our understanding of God, truth, revelation
and reason. 6 x 9, 224 pp, HC, 978-1-58023-411-5 **$24.99**

The Death of Death: Resurrection and Immortality in Jewish Thought
By Rabbi Neil Gillman, PhD 6 x 9, 336 pp, Quality PB, 978-1-58023-081-0 **$18.95**

Doing Jewish Theology: God, Torah & Israel in Modern Judaism *By Rabbi Neil Gillman, PhD*
6 x 9, 304 pp, Quality PB, 978-1-58023-439-9 **$18.99**; HC, 978-1-58023-322-4 **$24.99**

Ethics of the Sages: *Pirke Avot—Annotated & Explained*
Translation & Annotation by Rabbi Rami Shapiro 5½ x 8½, 192 pp, Quality PB, 978-1-59473-207-2 **$16.99***

Hasidic Tales: Annotated & Explained *Translation & Annotation by Rabbi Rami Shapiro*
5½ x 8½, 240 pp, Quality PB, 978-1-893361-86-7 **$16.95***

A Heart of Many Rooms: Celebrating the Many Voices within Judaism
By Dr. David Hartman 6 x 9, 352 pp, Quality PB, 978-1-58023-156-5 **$19.95**

The Hebrew Prophets: Selections Annotated & Explained
Translation & Annotation by Rabbi Rami Shapiro; Foreword by Rabbi Zalman M. Schachter-Shalomi
5½ x 8½, 224 pp, Quality PB, 978-1-59473-037-5 **$16.99***

A Jewish Understanding of the New Testament *By Rabbi Samuel Sandmel;
Preface by Rabbi David Sandmel* 5½ x 8½, 368 pp, Quality PB, 978-1-59473-048-1 **$19.99***

Jews and Judaism in the 21st Century: Human Responsibility, the Presence of God
and the Future of the Covenant *Edited by Rabbi Edward Feinstein; Foreword by Paula E. Hyman*
6 x 9, 192 pp, Quality PB, 978-1-58023-374-3 **$19.99**; HC, 978-1-58023-315-6 **$24.99**

A Living Covenant: The Innovative Spirit in Traditional Judaism
By Dr. David Hartman 6 x 9, 368 pp, Quality PB, 978-1-58023-011-7 **$25.00**

Love and Terror in the God Encounter: The Theological Legacy of Rabbi Joseph
B. Soloveitchik *By Dr. David Hartman* 6 x 9, 240 pp, Quality PB, 978-1-58023-176-3 **$19.95**

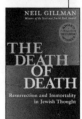

The Personhood of God: Biblical Theology, Human Faith and the Divine Image
By Dr. Yochanan Muffs; Foreword by Dr. David Hartman
6 x 9, 240 pp, Quality PB, 978-1-58023-338-5 **$18.99**; HC, 978-1-58023-265-4 **$24.99**

A Touch of the Sacred: A Theologian's Informal Guide to Jewish Belief
By Dr. Eugene B. Borowitz and Frances W. Schwartz
6 x 9, 256 pp, Quality PB, 978-1-58023-416-0 **$16.99**; HC, 978-1-58023-337-8 **$21.99**

Traces of God: Seeing God in Torah, History and Everyday Life *By Rabbi Neil Gillman, PhD*
6 x 9, 240 pp, Quality PB, 978-1-58023-369-9 **$16.99**

We Jews and Jesus: Exploring Theological Differences for Mutual Understanding *By Rabbi
Samuel Sandmel; Preface by Rabbi David Sandmel* 6 x 9, 192 pp, Quality PB, 978-1-59473-208-9 **$16.99***

Your Word Is Fire: The Hasidic Masters on Contemplative Prayer
Edited and translated by Rabbi Arthur Green, PhD, and Barry W. Holtz
6 x 9, 160 pp, Quality PB, 978-1-879045-25-5 **$15.95**

I Am Jewish
Personal Reflections Inspired by the Last Words of Daniel Pearl
Almost 150 Jews—both famous and not—from all walks of life, from all around
the world, write about many aspects of their Judaism.
Edited by Judea and Ruth Pearl 6 x 9, 304 pp, Deluxe PB w/ flaps, 978-1-58023-259-3 **$18.99**
Download a free copy of the *I Am Jewish Teacher's Guide* at www.jewishlights.com.

Hannah Senesh: Her Life and Diary, The First Complete Edition
By Hannah Senesh; Foreword by Marge Piercy; Preface by Eitan Senesh; Afterword by Roberta Grossman
6 x 9, 368 pp, b/w photos, Quality PB, 978-1-58023-342-2 **$19.99**

*A book from SkyLight Paths, Jewish Lights' sister imprint

Spirituality/Prayer

Making Prayer Real: Leading Jewish Spiritual Voices on Why Prayer Is Difficult and What to Do about It *By Rabbi Mike Comins*
A new and different response to the challenges of Jewish prayer, with "best prayer practices" from Jewish spiritual leaders of all denominations.
6 x 9, 320 pp, Quality PB, 978-1-58023-417-7 **$18.99**

Witnesses to the One: The Spiritual History of the *Sh'ma*
By Rabbi Joseph B. Meszler; Foreword by Rabbi Elyse Goldstein
6 x 9, 176 pp, Quality PB, 978-1-58023-400-9 **$16.99**; HC, 978-1-58023-309-5 **$19.99**

My People's Prayer Book Series: Traditional Prayers, Modern Commentaries *Edited by Rabbi Lawrence A. Hoffman, PhD*
Provides diverse and exciting commentary to the traditional liturgy. Will help you find new wisdom in Jewish prayer, and bring liturgy into your life. Each book includes Hebrew text, modern translations and commentaries from all perspectives of the Jewish world.

Vol. 1—The *Sh'ma* and Its Blessings
7 x 10, 168 pp, HC, 978-1-879045-79-8 **$24.99**
Vol. 2—The *Amidah* 7 x 10, 240 pp, HC, 978-1-879045-80-4 **$24.95**
Vol. 3—*P'sukei D'zimrah* (Morning Psalms)
7 x 10, 240 pp, HC, 978-1-879045-81-1 **$29.99**
Vol. 4—*Seder K'riat Hatorah* (The Torah Service)
7 x 10, 264 pp, HC, 978-1-879045-82-8 **$23.95**
Vol. 5—*Birkhot Hashachar* (Morning Blessings)
7 x 10, 240 pp, HC, 978-1-879045-83-5 **$24.95**
Vol. 6—*Tachanun* and Concluding Prayers
7 x 10, 240 pp, HC, 978-1-879045-84-2 **$24.95**
Vol. 7—Shabbat at Home 7 x 10, 240 pp, HC, 978-1-879045-85-9 **$24.95**
Vol. 8—*Kabbalat Shabbat* (Welcoming Shabbat in the Synagogue)
7 x 10, 240 pp, HC, 978-1-58023-121-3 **$24.99**
Vol. 9—Welcoming the Night: *Minchah* and *Ma'ariv* (Afternoon and Evening Prayer) 7 x 10, 272 pp, HC, 978-1-58023-262-3 **$24.99**
Vol. 10—Shabbat Morning: *Shacharit* and *Musaf* (Morning and Additional Services) 7 x 10, 240 pp, HC, 978-1-58023-240-1 **$24.99**

Spirituality/Lawrence Kushner

I'm God;You're Not: Observations on Organized Religion & Other Disguises of the Ego
6 x 9, 256 pp, HC, 978-1-58023-441-2 **$21.99**

The Book of Letters: A Mystical Hebrew Alphabet
Popular HC Edition, 6 x 9, 80 pp, 2-color text, 978-1-879045-00-2 **$24.95**
Collector's Limited Edition, 9 x 12, 80 pp, gold-foil-embossed pages, w/ limited-edition silkscreened print, 978-1-879045-04-0 **$349.00**

The Book of Miracles: A Young Person's Guide to Jewish Spiritual Awareness
6 x 9, 96 pp, 2-color illus., HC, 978-1-879045-78-1 **$16.95** *For ages 9–13*

The Book of Words: Talking Spiritual Life, Living Spiritual Talk
6 x 9, 160 pp, Quality PB, 978-1-58023-020-9 **$18.99**

Eyes Remade for Wonder: A Lawrence Kushner Reader *Introduction by Thomas Moore*
6 x 9, 240 pp, Quality PB, 978-1-58023-042-1 **$18.95**

God Was in This Place & I, i Did Not Know: Finding Self, Spirituality and Ultimate Meaning 6 x 9, 192 pp, Quality PB, 978-1-879045-33-0 **$16.95**

Honey from the Rock: An Introduction to Jewish Mysticism
6 x 9, 176 pp, Quality PB, 978-1-58023-073-5 **$16.95**

Invisible Lines of Connection: Sacred Stories of the Ordinary
5½ x 8½, 160 pp, Quality PB, 978-1-879045-98-9 **$15.95**

Jewish Spirituality: A Brief Introduction for Christians
5½ x 8½, 112 pp, Quality PB, 978-1-58023-150-3 **$12.95**

The River of Light: Jewish Mystical Awareness
6 x 9, 192 pp, Quality PB, 978-1-58023-096-4 **$16.95**

The Way Into Jewish Mystical Tradition
6 x 9, 224 pp, Quality PB, 978-1-58023-200-5 **$18.99**; HC, 978-1-58023-029-2 **$21.95**

Meditation

Jewish Meditation Practices for Everyday Life
Awakening Your Heart, Connecting with God
By Rabbi Jeff Roth
Offers a fresh take on meditation that draws on life experience and living life with
greater clarity as opposed to the traditional method of rigorous study.
6 x 9, 224 pp, Quality PB, 978-1-58023-397-2 **$18.99**

The Handbook of Jewish Meditation Practices
A Guide for Enriching the Sabbath and Other Days of Your Life
By Rabbi David A. Cooper Easy-to-learn meditation techniques.
6 x 9, 208 pp, Quality PB, 978-1-58023-102-2 **$16.95**

Discovering Jewish Meditation: Instruction & Guidance for Learning an Ancient
Spiritual Practice *By Nan Fink Gefen, PhD* 6 x 9, 208 pp, Quality PB, 978-1-58023-067-4 **$16.95**

Meditation from the Heart of Judaism: Today's Teachers Share Their Practices,
Techniques, and Faith *Edited by Avram Davis*
6 x 9, 256 pp, Quality PB, 978-1-58023-049-0 **$16.95**

Ritual/Sacred Practices

The Jewish Dream Book: The Key to Opening the Inner Meaning of
Your Dreams *By Vanessa L. Ochs, PhD, with Elizabeth Ochs; Illus. by Kristina Swarner*
Instructions for how modern people can perform ancient Jewish dream practices
and dream interpretations drawn from the Jewish wisdom tradition.
8 x 8, 128 pp, Full-color illus., Deluxe PB w/ flaps, 978-1-58023-132-9 **$16.95**

God in Your Body: Kabbalah, Mindfulness and Embodied Spiritual Practice
By Jay Michaelson
The first comprehensive treatment of the body in Jewish spiritual practice and an
essential guide to the sacred.
6 x 9, 272 pp, Quality PB, 978-1-58023-304-0 **$18.99**

The Book of Jewish Sacred Practices: CLAL's Guide to Everyday &
Holiday Rituals & Blessings *Edited by Rabbi Irwin Kula and Vanessa L. Ochs, PhD*
6 x 9, 368 pp, Quality PB, 978-1-58023-152-7 **$18.95**

Jewish Ritual: A Brief Introduction for Christians
By Rabbi Kerry M. Olitzky and Rabbi Daniel Judson
5½ x 8½, 144 pp, Quality PB, 978-1-58023-210-4 **$14.99**

The Rituals & Practices of a Jewish Life: A Handbook for Personal Spiritual
Renewal *Edited by Rabbi Kerry M. Olitzky and Rabbi Daniel Judson*
6 x 9, 272 pp, Illus., Quality PB, 978-1-58023-169-5 **$18.95**

The Sacred Art of Lovingkindness: Preparing to Practice
By Rabbi Rami Shapiro 5½ x 8½, 176 pp, Quality PB, 978-1-59473-151-8 **$16.99**
(A book from SkyLight Paths, Jewish Lights' sister imprint)

Science Fiction/Mystery & Detective Fiction

Criminal Kabbalah: An Intriguing Anthology of Jewish Mystery &
Detective Fiction *Edited by Lawrence W. Raphael; Foreword by Laurie R. King*
All-new stories from twelve of today's masters of mystery and detective fiction—
sure to delight mystery buffs of all faith traditions.
6 x 9, 256 pp, Quality PB, 978-1-58023-109-1 **$16.95**

Mystery Midrash: An Anthology of Jewish Mystery & Detective Fiction
Edited by Lawrence W. Raphael; Preface by Joel Siegel
6 x 9, 304 pp, Quality PB, 978-1-58023-055-1 **$16.95**

Wandering Stars: An Anthology of Jewish Fantasy & Science Fiction
Edited by Jack Dann; Introduction by Isaac Asimov
6 x 9, 272 pp, Quality PB, 978-1-58023-005-6 **$18.99**

More Wandering Stars: An Anthology of Outstanding Stories of Jewish Fantasy and
Science Fiction *Edited by Jack Dann; Introduction by Isaac Asimov*
6 x 9, 192 pp, Quality PB, 978-1-58023-063-6 **$16.95**

Spirituality

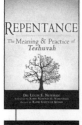

Repentance: The Meaning and Practice of *Teshuvah*
By Dr. Louis E. Newman; Foreword by Rabbi Harold M. Schulweis; Preface by Rabbi Karyn D. Kedar
Examines both the practical and philosophical dimensions of *teshuvah*, Judaism's core religious-moral teaching on repentance, and its value for us—Jews and non-Jews alike—today. 6 x 9, 256 pp, HC, 978-1-58023-426-9 **$24.99**

Tanya, the Masterpiece of Hasidic Wisdom
Selections Annotated & Explained
Translation & Annotation by Rabbi Rami Shapiro; Foreword by Rabbi Zalman M. Schachter-Shalomi
Brings the genius of *Tanya*, one of the most powerful books of Jewish wisdom, to anyone seeking to deepen their understanding of the soul.
5½ x 8½, 240 pp, Quality PB, 978-1-59473-275-1 **$16.99**
(A book from SkyLight Paths, Jewish Lights' sister imprint)

Aleph-Bet Yoga: Embodying the Hebrew Letters for Physical and Spiritual Well-Being
By Steven A. Rapp; Foreword by Tamar Frankiel, PhD, and Judy Greenfeld; Preface by Hart Lazer
7 x 10, 128 pp, b/w photos, Quality PB, Lay-flat binding, 978-1-58023-162-6 **$16.95**

A Book of Life: Embracing Judaism as a Spiritual Practice
By Rabbi Michael Strassfeld 6 x 9, 544 pp, Quality PB, 978-1-58023-247-0 **$19.99**

Bringing the Psalms to Life: How to Understand and Use the Book of Psalms
By Rabbi Daniel F. Polish, PhD 6 x 9, 208 pp, Quality PB, 978-1-58023-157-2 **$16.95**

Does the Soul Survive? A Jewish Journey to Belief in Afterlife, Past Lives & Living with Purpose *By Rabbi Elie Kaplan Spitz; Foreword by Brian L. Weiss, MD*
6 x 9, 288 pp, Quality PB, 978-1-58023-165-7 **$16.99**

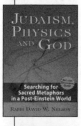

First Steps to a New Jewish Spirit: Reb Zalman's Guide to Recapturing the Intimacy & Ecstasy in Your Relationship with God *By Rabbi Zalman M. Schachter-Shalomi with Donald Gropman* 6 x 9, 144 pp, Quality PB, 978-1-58023-182-4 **$16.95**

Foundations of Sephardic Spirituality: The Inner Life of Jews of the Ottoman Empire
By Rabbi Marc D. Angel, PhD 6 x 9, 224 pp, Quality PB, 978-1-58023-341-5 **$18.99**

God & the Big Bang: Discovering Harmony between Science & Spirituality
By Dr. Daniel C. Matt 6 x 9, 216 pp, Quality PB, 978-1-879045-89-7 **$16.99**

God in Our Relationships: Spirituality between People from the Teachings of Martin Buber *By Rabbi Dennis S. Ross* 5½ x 8½, 160 pp, Quality PB, 978-1-58023-147-3 **$16.95**

The Jewish Lights Spirituality Handbook: A Guide to Understanding, Exploring & Living a Spiritual Life *Edited by Stuart M. Matlins*
What exactly is "Jewish" about spirituality? How do I make it a part of my life? Fifty of today's foremost spiritual leaders share their ideas and experience with us.
6 x 9, 456 pp, Quality PB, 978-1-58023-093-3 **$19.99**

Judaism, Physics and God: Searching for Sacred Metaphors in a Post-Einstein World
By Rabbi David W. Nelson 6 x 9, 352 pp, Quality PB, inc. reader's discussion guide, 978-1-58023-306-4 **$18.99**; HC, 352 pp, 978-1-58023-252-4 **$24.99**

Meaning & Mitzvah: Daily Practices for Reclaiming Judaism through Prayer, God, Torah, Hebrew, Mitzvot and Peoplehood *By Rabbi Goldie Milgram*
7 x 9, 336 pp, Quality PB, 978-1-58023-256-2 **$19.99**

Minding the Temple of the Soul: Balancing Body, Mind, and Spirit through Traditional Jewish Prayer, Movement, and Meditation *By Tamar Frankiel, PhD, and Judy Greenfeld*
7 x 10, 184 pp, Illus., Quality PB, 978-1-879045-64-4 **$18.99**

One God Clapping: The Spiritual Path of a Zen Rabbi *By Rabbi Alan Lew with Sherril Jaffe*
5½ x 8½, 336 pp, Quality PB, 978-1-58023-115-2 **$16.95**

The Soul of the Story: Meetings with Remarkable People
By Rabbi David Zeller 6 x 9, 288 pp, HC, 978-1-58023-272-2 **$21.99**

There Is No Messiah ... and You're It: The Stunning Transformation of Judaism's Most Provocative Idea *By Rabbi Robert N. Levine, DD*
6 x 9, 192 pp, Quality PB, 978-1-58023-255-5 **$16.99**

These Are the Words: A Vocabulary of Jewish Spiritual Life
By Rabbi Arthur Green, PhD 6 x 9, 304 pp, Quality PB, 978-1-58023-107-7 **$18.95**

Inspiration

The Seven Questions You're Asked in Heaven: Reviewing and Renewing Your Life on Earth *By Dr. Ron Wolfson*
An intriguing and entertaining resource for living a life that matters.
6 x 9, 176 pp, Quality PB, 978-1-58023-407-8 **$16.99**

Happiness and the Human Spirit: The Spirituality of Becoming the Best You Can Be *By Rabbi Abraham J. Twerski, MD*
Shows you that true happiness is attainable once you stop looking outside yourself for the source. 6 x 9, 176 pp, Quality PB, 978-1-58023-404-7 **$16.99**; HC, 978-1-58023-343-9 **$19.99**

A Formula for Proper Living: Practical Lessons from Life and Torah
By Rabbi Abraham J. Twerski, MD
Gives you practical lessons for life that you can put to day-to-day use in dealing with yourself and others. 6 x 9, 144 pp, HC, 978-1-58023-402-3 **$19.99**

The Bridge to Forgiveness: Stories and Prayers for Finding God and Restoring Wholeness *By Rabbi Karyn D. Kedar* 6 x 9, 176 pp, HC, 978-1-58023-324-8 **$19.99**

The Empty Chair: Finding Hope and Joy—Timeless Wisdom from a Hasidic Master, Rebbe Nachman of Breslov *Adapted by Moshe Mykoff and the Breslov Research Institute*
4 x 6, 128 pp, Deluxe PB w/ flaps, 978-1-879045-67-5 **$9.99**

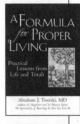

The Gentle Weapon: Prayers for Everyday and Not-So-Everyday Moments—Timeless Wisdom from the Teachings of the Hasidic Master, Rebbe Nachman of Breslov *Adapted by Moshe Mykoff and S. C. Mizrahi, together with the Breslov Research Institute*
4 x 6, 144 pp, Deluxe PB w/ flaps, 978-1-58023-022-3 **$9.99**

God Whispers: Stories of the Soul, Lessons of the Heart *By Rabbi Karyn D. Kedar*
6 x 9, 176 pp, Quality PB, 978-1-58023-088-9 **$15.95**

God's To-Do List: 103 Ways to Be an Angel and Do God's Work on Earth
By Dr. Ron Wolfson 6 x 9, 144 pp, Quality PB, 978-1-58023-301-9 **$16.99**

Jewish Stories from Heaven and Earth: Inspiring Tales to Nourish the Heart and Soul *Edited by Rabbi Dov Peretz Elkins* 6 x 9, 304 pp, Quality PB, 978-1-58023-363-7 **$16.99**

Life's Daily Blessings: Inspiring Reflections on Gratitude and Joy for Every Day, Based on Jewish Wisdom *By Rabbi Kerry M. Olitzky* 4½ x 6¼, 368 pp, Quality PB, 978-1-58023-396-5 **$16.99**

Restful Reflections: Nighttime Inspiration to Calm the Soul, Based on Jewish Wisdom *By Rabbi Kerry M. Olitzky and Rabbi Lori Forman* 4½ x 6¼, 448 pp, Quality PB, 978-1-58023-091-9 **$15.95**

Sacred Intentions: Daily Inspiration to Strengthen the Spirit, Based on Jewish Wisdom *By Rabbi Kerry M. Olitzky and Rabbi Lori Forman* 4½ x 6¼, 448 pp, Quality PB, 978-1-58023-061-2 **$15.95**

Kabbalah/Mysticism

Ehyeh: A Kabbalah for Tomorrow
By Rabbi Arthur Green, PhD 6 x 9, 224 pp, Quality PB, 978-1-58023-213-5 **$18.99**

The Flame of the Heart: Prayers of a Chasidic Mystic
By Reb Noson of Breslov; Translated and adapted by David Sears, with the Breslov Research Institute
5 x 7¼, 160 pp, Quality PB, 978-1-58023-246-3 **$15.99**

The Gift of Kabbalah: Discovering the Secrets of Heaven, Renewing Your Life on Earth
By Tamar Frankiel, PhD 6 x 9, 256 pp, Quality PB, 978-1-58023-141-1 **$16.95**

Kabbalah: A Brief Introduction for Christians
By Tamar Frankiel, PhD 5½ x 8½, 208 pp, Quality PB, 978-1-58023-303-3 **$16.99**

The Lost Princess & Other Kabbalistic Tales of Rebbe Nachman of Breslov
The Seven Beggars & Other Kabbalistic Tales of Rebbe Nachman of Breslov
Translated by Rabbi Aryeh Kaplan; Preface by Rabbi Chaim Kramer
Lost Princess: 6 x 9, 400 pp, Quality PB, 978-1-58023-217-3 **$18.99**
Seven Beggars: 6 x 9, 192 pp, Quality PB, 978-1-58023-250-0 **$16.99**

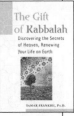

Seek My Face: A Jewish Mystical Theology *By Rabbi Arthur Green, PhD*
6 x 9, 304 pp, Quality PB, 978-1-58023-130-5 **$19.95**

Zohar: Annotated & Explained *Translation & Annotation by Dr. Daniel C. Matt; Foreword by Andrew Harvey* 5½ x 8½, 176 pp, Quality PB, 978-1-893361-51-5 **$15.99**
(A book from SkyLight Paths, Jewish Lights' sister imprint)

See also *The Way Into Jewish Mystical Tradition* in The Way Into... Series.

About Jewish Lights

People of all faiths and backgrounds yearn for books that attract, engage, educate, and spiritually inspire.

Our principal goal is to stimulate thought and help all people learn about who the Jewish People are, where they come from, and what the future can be made to hold. While people of our diverse Jewish heritage are the primary audience, our books speak to people in the Christian world as well and will broaden their understanding of Judaism and the roots of their own faith.

We bring to you authors who are at the forefront of spiritual thought and experience. While each has something different to say, they all say it in a voice that you can hear.

Our books are designed to welcome you and then to engage, stimulate, and inspire. We judge our success not only by whether or not our books are beautiful and commercially successful, but by whether or not they make a difference in your life.

For your information and convenience, at the back of this book we have provided a list of other Jewish Lights books you might find interesting and useful. They cover all the categories of your life:

Bar/Bat Mitzvah
Bible Study / Midrash
Children's Books
Congregation Resources
Current Events / History
Ecology / Environment
Fiction: Mystery, Science Fiction
Grief / Healing
Holidays / Holy Days
Inspiration
Kabbalah / Mysticism / Enneagram

Life Cycle
Meditation
Men's Interest
Parenting
Prayer / Ritual / Sacred Practice
Social Justice
Spirituality
Theology / Philosophy
Travel
Twelve Steps
Women's Interest

Stuart M. Matlins, Publisher

Or phone, fax, mail or e-mail to: **JEWISH LIGHTS Publishing**
Sunset Farm Offices, Route 4 • P.O. Box 237 • Woodstock, Vermont 05091
Tel: (802) 457-4000 • Fax: (802) 457-4004 • www.jewishlights.com
Credit card orders: (800) 962-4544 (8:30AM–5:30PM ET Monday–Friday)
Generous discounts on quantity orders. SATISFACTION GUARANTEED. Prices subject to change.

For more information about each book, visit our website at www.jewishlights.com